The Muses Elizium by Michael Drayton

Michael Drayton was born in 1563 at Hartshill, near Nuneaton, Warwickshire, England. The facts of his early life remain unknown.

Drayton first published, in 1590, a volume of spiritual poems; The Harmony of the Church. Ironically the Archbishop of Canterbury seized almost the entire edition and had it destroyed.

In 1593 he published Idea: The Shepherd's Garland, 9 pastorals celebrating his own love-sorrows under the poetic name of Rowland. This was later expanded to a 64 sonnet cycle.

With the publication of The Legend of Piers Gaveston, Matilda and Mortimeriados, later enlarged and re-published, in 1603, under the title of The Barons' Wars. His career began to gather interest and attention.

In 1596, The Legend of Robert, Duke of Normandy, another historical poem was published, followed in 1597 by England's Heroical Epistles, a series of historical studies, in imitation of those of Ovid. Written in the heroic couplet, they contain some of his finest writing.

Like other poets of his era, Drayton wrote for the theatre; but unlike Shakespeare, Jonson, or Samuel Daniel, he invested little of his art in the genre. Between 1597 and 1602, Drayton was a member of the stable of playwrights who worked for Philip Henslowe. Henslowe's Diary links Drayton's name with 23 plays from that period, and, for all but one unfinished work, in collaboration with others such as Thomas Dekker, Anthony Munday, and Henry Chettle. Only one play has survived; Part 1 of Sir John Oldcastle, which Drayton wrote with Munday, Robert Wilson, and Richard Hathwaye but little of Drayton can be seen in its pages.

By this time, as a poet, Drayton was well received and admired at the Court of Elizabeth 1st. If he hoped to continue that admiration with the accession of James 1st he thought wrong. In 1603, he addressed a poem of compliment to James I, but it was ridiculed, and his services rudely rejected.

In 1605 Drayton reprinted his most important works; the historical poems and the Idea. Also published was a fantastic satire called The Man in the Moon and, for the for the first time the famous Ballad of Agincourt.

Since 1598 he had worked on Poly-Olbion, a work to celebrate all the points of topographical or antiquarian interest in Great Britain. Eighteen books in total, the first were published in 1614 and the last in 1622.

In 1627 he published another of his miscellaneous volumes. In it Drayton printed The Battle of Agincourt (an historical poem but not to be confused with his ballad on the same subject), The Miseries of Queen Margaret, and the acclaimed Nimphidia, the Court of Faery, as well as several other important pieces.

Drayton last published in 1630 with The Muses' Elizium.

Michael Drayton died in London on December 23rd, 1631. He was buried in Westminster Abbey, in Poets' Corner. A monument was placed there with memorial lines attributed to Ben Jonson.

Index of Contents

THE MUSES ELIZIUM

The Description of Elizium

A Paradise on earth is found,
Though farre from vulgar sight,
Which with those pleasures doth abound
That it Elizium hight.

Where, in Delights that never fade,
The Muses lulled be,
And sit at pleasure in the shade
Of many a stately tree,

Which no rough Tempest makes to reele
Nor their straight bodies bowes,
Their lofty tops doe never feele
The weight of winters snowes;

In Groves that evermore are greene,
No falling leafe is there,
But Philomel (of birds the Queene)
In Musicke spends the yeare.

The Merle upon her mertle Perch,
There to the Mavis sings,
Who from the top of some curld Berch
Those notes redoubled rings;

There Daysyes damaske every place
Nor once their beauties lose,
That when proud Phœbus hides his face
Themselves they scorne to close.

The Pansy and the Violet here,
As seeming to descend,
Both from one Root, a very payre,
For sweetnesse yet contend,

And pointing to a Pinke to tell
Which beares it, it is loath,
To judge it; but replyes for smell
That it excels them both.

Wherewith displeasde they hang their heads
So angry soone they grow
And from their odoriferous beds
Their sweets at it they throw.

The winter here a Summer is,
No waste is made by time,
Nor doth the Autumne ever misse
The blossomes of the Prime.

The flower that Iuly forth doth bring
In Aprill here is seene,
The Primrose that puts on the Spring
In July decks each Greene.

The sweets for soveraignty contend
And so abundant be,
That to the very Earth they lend

And Barke of every Tree:

Rills rising out of every Banck,
In wild Meanders strayne,
And playing many a wanton pranck
Vpon the speckled plaine,

In Gambols and lascivious Gyres
Their time they still bestow
Nor to their Fountaines none retyres,
Nor on their course will goe.

Those Brooks with Lillies bravely deckt,
So proud and wanton made,
That they their courses quite neglect:
And seeme as though they stayde,

Faire Flora in her state to viewe
Which through those Lillies looks,
Or as those Lillies leand to shew
Their beauties to the brooks.

That Phœbusin his lofty race,
Oft layes aside his beames
And comes to coole his glowing face
In these delicious streames;

Oft spreading Vines clime up the Cleeues,
Whose ripned clusters there,
Their liquid purple drop, which driues
A Vintage through the yeere.

Those Cleeues whose craggy sides are clad
With Trees of sundry sutes,
Which make continuall summer glad,
Euen bending with their fruits,

Some ripening, ready some to fall,
Some blossom'd, some to bloome,
Like gorgeous hangings on the wall
Of some rich princely Roome:

Pomegranates, Lymons, Cytrons, so
Their laded branches bow,
Their leaves in number that outgoe
Nor roomth will them alow.

There in perpetuall Summers shade,

Apolloes Prophets sit,
Among the flowres that never fade,
But flowrish like their wit;

To whom the Nimphes upon their Lyres,
Tune many a curious lay,
And with their most melodious Quires
Make short the longest day.

The thrice three Virgins heavenly Cleere,
Their trembling Timbrels sound,
Whilst the three comely Graces there
Dance many a dainty Round,

Decay nor Age there nothing knowes,
There is continuall Youth,
As Time on plant or creatures growes,
So still their strength renewth.

The Poets Paradice this is,
To which but few can come;
The Muses onely bower of blisse
Their Deare Elizium.

Here happy soules, (their blessed bowers,
Free from the rude resort
Of beastly people) spend the houres,
In harmelesse mirth and sport,

Then on to the Elizian plaines
Apollo doth invite you
Where he provides with pastorall straines,
In Nimphals to delight you.

THE FIRST NIMPHALL

RODOPE and DORIDA

This Nimphall of delights doth treat,
Choice beauties, and proportions neat,
Of curious shapes, and dainty features
Describd in two most perfect creatures.

When Phœbus with a face of mirth,
Had flung abroad his beames,
To blanch the bosome of the earth,

And glaze the gliding streames.
Within a goodly Mertle grove,
Upon that hallowed day
The Nimphes to the bright Queene of love
Their vowes were usde to pay.
Faire Rodope and Dorida
Met in those sacred shades,
Then whom the Sunne in all his way,
Nere saw two daintier Maids.
And through the thickets thrild his fires,
Supposing to have seene
The soveraigne Goddesse of desires,
Or loves Emperious Queene:
Both of so wondrous beauties were,
In shape both so excell,
That to be paraleld elsewhere,
No judging eye could tell.
And their affections so surpasse,
As well it might be deemd,
That th' one of them the other was,
And but themselves they seem'd.
And whilst the Nimphes that neare this place,
Disposed were to play
At Barly-breake and Prison-base,
Doe passe the time away:
This peerlesse payre together set,
The other at their sport,
None neare their free discourse to let,
Each other thus they court,

DORIDA - My sweet, my soveraigne Rodope,
My deare delight, my love,
That Locke of hayre thou sentst to me,
I to this Bracelet wove;
Which brighter every day doth grow
The longer it is worne,
As its delicious fellowes doe,
Thy Temples that adorne.

RODOPE - Nay had I thine my Dorida,
I would them so bestow,
As that the winde upon my way,
Might backward make them flow,
So should it in its greatst excesse
Turne to becalmed ayre,
And quite forget all boistrousnesse
To play with every hayre.

DORIDA - To me like thine had nature given,
A Brow, so Archt, so cleere,
A Front, wherein so much of heaven
Doth to each eye appeare,
The world should see, I would strike dead
The Milky Way that's now,
And say that Nectar Hebe shed
Fell all upon my Brow.

RODOPE - O had I eyes like Doridaes,
I would inchant the day
And make the Sunne to stand at gaze,
Till he forget his way:
And cause his Sister Queene of Streames,
When so I list by night;
By her much blushing at my Beames
T' eclipse her borrowed light.

DORIDA - Had I a Cheeke like Rodopes,
In midst of which doth stand,
A Grove of Roses, such as these,
In such a snowy land:
I would then make the Lilly which we now
So much for whitenesse name,
As drooping downe the head to bow,
And die for very shame.

RODOPE - Had I a bosome like to thine,
When I it pleas'd to show,
T' what part o' th' Skie I would incline
I would make th' Etheriall bowe,
My swannish breast brancht all with blew,
In bravery like the spring:
In Winter to the generall view
Full Summer forth should bring.

DORIDA - Had I a body like my deare,
Were I so straight so tall,
O, if so broad my shoulders were,
Had I a waste so small;
I would challenge the proud Queene of love
To yeeld to me for shape,
And I should feare that Mars or Iove
Would venter for my rape.

RODOPE - Had I a hand like thee my Gerle,
(This hand O let me kisse)
These Ivory Arrowes pyl'd with pearle,

Had I a hand like this;
I would not doubt at all to make,
Each finger of my hand
To taske swift Mercury to take
With his inchanting wand.

DORIDA - Had I a Theigh like Rodopes;
Which twas my chance to viewe,
When lying on yon banck at ease,
The wind thy skirt up blew,
I would say it were a columne wrought
To some intent Diuine,
And for our chaste Diana sought,
A pillar for her shryne.

RODOPE - Had I a Leg but like to thine
That were so neat, so cleane,
A swelling Calfe, a Small so fine,
An Ankle, round and leane,
I would tell nature she doth misse
Her old skill; and maintaine,
She shewd her master peece in this,
Not to be done againe.

DORIDA - Had I that Foot hid in those shoos,
(Proportion'd to my height)
Short Heele, thin Instep, even Toes,
A Sole so wondrous straight,
The Forresters and Nimphes at this
Amazed all should stand,
And kneeling downe, should meekely kisse
The Print left in the sand.

By this the Nimphes came from their sport,
All pleased wondrous well,
And to these Maydens make report
What lately them befell:
One said the dainty Lelipa
Did all the rest out-goe,
Another would a wager lay
She would outstrip a Roe;
Sayes one, how like you Florimel
There is your dainty face:
A fourth replide, she lik't that well,
Yet better lik't her grace,
She's counted, I confesse, quoth she,
To be our onely Pearle,
Yet have I heard her oft to be

A melancholy Gerle.
Another said she quite mistoke,
That onely was her art,
When melancholly had her looke
Then mirth was in her heart;
And hath she then that pretty trick
Another doth reply,
I thought no Nimph could have bin sick
Of that disease but I;
I know you can dissemble well
Quoth one to give you due,
But here be some (who Ile not tell)
Can do't as well as you,
Who thus replies, I know that too,
We have it from our Mother,
Yet there be some this thing can doe
More cunningly then other:
If Maydens but dissemble can
Their sorrow and ther ioy,
Their pore dissimulation than,
Is but a very toy.

THE SECOND NIMPHALL

LALUS, CLEON, and LIROPE

The Muse new Courtship doth deuise,
By Natures strange Varieties,
Whose Rarieties she here relates,
And gives you Pastorall Delicates.

Lalus a lolly youthfull Lad,
With Cleon, no lesse crown'd
With vertues; both their beings had
On the Elizian ground.
Both having parts so excellent,
That it a question was,
Which should be the most eminent,
Or did in ought surpasse:
This Cleon was a Mountaineer,
And of the wilder kinde,
And from his birth had many a yeere
Bin nurst up by a Hinde.
And as the sequell well did show,
It very well might be;
For never Hart, nor Hare, nor Roe,

Were halfe so swift as he.
But Lalus in the Vale was bred,
Amongst the Sheepe and Neate,
And by these Nimphes there choicly fed,
With Hony, Milke, and Wheate;
Of Stature goodly, faire of speech,
And of behauiour mylde,
Like those there in the Valley rich,
That bred him of a chyld.
Of Falconry they had the skill,
Their Halkes to feed and flye,
No better Hunters ere clome Hill,
Nor hollowed to a Cry:
In Dingles deepe, and Mountains hore,
Oft with the bearded Speare
They combated the tusky Boare,
And slew the angry Beare.
In Musicke they were wondrous quaint,
Fine Aers they could deuise;
They very curiously could Paint,
And neatly Poetize;
That wagers many time were laid
On Questions that arose,
Which song the witty Lalus made,
Which Cleon should compose.
The stately Steed they manag'd well,
Of Fence the art they knew,
For Dansing they did all excell
The Gerles that to them drew;
To throw the Sledge, to pitch the Barre,
To wrestle and to Run,
They all the Youth exceld so farre,
That still the Prize they wonne.
These sprightly Gallants lou'd a Lasse,
Cald Lirope the bright,
In the whole world there scarcely was
So delicate a Wight,
There was no Beauty so diuine
That ever Nimph did grace,
But it beyond it selfe did shine
In her more heavenly face:
What forme she pleasd each thing would take
That ere she did behold,
Of Pebbles she could Diamonds make,
Grosse Iron turne to Gold:
Such power there with her presence came
Sterne Tempests she alayd,
The cruell Tiger she could tame,

She raging Torrents staid,
She chid, she cherisht, she gave life,
Againe she made to dye,
She raisd a warre, apeasd a Strife,
With turning of her eye.
Some said a God did her beget,
But much deceiu'd were they,
Her Father was a Riuelet,
Her Mother was a Fay.
Her Lineaments so fine that were,
She from the Fayrie tooke,
Her Beauties and Complection cleere,
By nature from the Brooke.
These Ryualls wayting for the houre
(The weather calme and faire)
When as she us'd to leave her Bower
To take the pleasant ayre
Acosting her; their complement
To her their Goddesse done;
By gifts they tempt her to consent,
When Lalus thus begun.

LALUS - Sweet Lirope I have a Lambe
Newly wayned from the Damme,
Of the right kinde, it is notted.
Naturally with purple spotted,
Into laughter it will put you,
To see how prettily 'twill But you;
When on sporting it is set,
It will beate you a Corvet,
And at every nimble bound
Turne it selfe above the ground;
When tis hungry it will bleate,
From your hand to have its meate,
And when it hath fully fed,
It will fetch lumpes above your head,
As innocently to expresse
Its silly sheepish thankfullnesse,
When you bid it, it will play,
Be it either night or day,
This Lirope I have for thee,
So thou alone wilt liue with me.

CLEON - From him O turne thine eare away,
And heare me my lou'd Lirope,
I have a Kid as white as milke,
His skin as soft as Naples silke,
His hornes in length are wondrous even,

And curiously by nature writhen;
It is of th' Arcadian kinde,
Ther's not the like twixt either Inde;
If you walke, 'twill walke you by,
If you sit downe, it downe will lye,
It with gesture will you wooe,
And counterfeit those things you doe;
Ore each Hillock it will vault,
And nimbly doe the Summer-sault,
Upon the hinder Legs 'twill goe,
And follow you a furlong so,
And if by chance a Tune you roate,
'Twill foote it finely to your note,
Seeke the worlde and you may misse
To finde out such a thing as this;
This my love I have for thee
So thou'lt leave him and goe with me.

LIROPE - Beleeve me Youths your gifts are rare,
And you offer wondrous faire;
Lalus for Lambe, Cleon for Kyd,
'Tis hard to judge which most doth bid,
And have you two such things in store,
And I n'er knew of them before?
Well yet I dare a Wager lay
That Brag my little Dog shall play,
As dainty tricks when I shall bid,
As Lalus Lambe, or Cleons Kid.
But t' may fall out that I may neede them
Till when yee may doe well to feed them;
Your Goate and Mutton pretty be
But Youths these are noe bayts for me,
Alasse good men, in vaine ye wooe,
'Tis not your Lambe nor Kid will doe.

LALUS - I have two Sparrowes white as Snow,
Whose pretty eyes like sparkes doe show;
In her Bosome Venus hatcht them
Where her little Cupid watcht them,
Till they too fledge their Nests forsooke
Themselves and to the Fields betooke,
Where by chance a Fowler caught them
Of whom I full dearely bought them;
They'll fetch you Conserve from the Hip,
And lay it softly on your Lip,
Through their nibling bills they'll Chirup
And fluttering feed you with the Sirup,
And if thence you put them by

They to your white necke will flye,
And if you expulse them there
They'll hang upon your braded Hayre;
You so long shall see them prattle
Till at length they'll fall to battle,
And when they have fought their fill,
You will smile to see them bill
These birds my Lirope's shall be
So thou'lt leave him and goe with me.

CLEON - His Sparrowes are not worth a rush
I'le finde as good in every bush,
Of Doves I have a dainty paire
Which when you please to take the Air,
About your head shall gently hover
You Cleere browe from the Sunne to cover,
And with their nimble wings shall fan you,
That neither Cold nor Heate shall tan you,
And like Vmbrellas with their feathers
Sheeld you in all sorts of weathers:
They be most dainty Coloured things,
They have Damask backs and Chequerd wings,
Their neckes more Various Cullours showe
Then there be mixed in the Bowe;
Venus saw the lesser Dove
And therewith was farre in Love,
Offering for't her goulden Ball
For her Sonne to play withall;
These my Liropes shall be
So shee'll leave him and goe with me.

LIROPE - Then for Sparrowes, and for Doves
I am fitted twixt my Loves,
But Lalus I take no delight
In Sparowes, for they'll scratch and bite
And though ioynd, they are ever wooing
Always billing, if not doeing,
Twixt Venus breasts if they have lyen
I much feare they'll infect myne;
Cleon your Doves are very dainty,
Tame Pidgeons else you know are plenty,
These may winne some of your Marrowes
I am not caught with Doves, nor Sparrowes,
I thanke ye kindly for your Coste,
Yet your labour is but loste.

LALUS - With full-leav'd Lillies I will stick
Thy braded hayre all o'r so thick,

That from it a Light shall throw
Like the Sunnes upon the Snow.
Thy Mantle shall be Violet Leaves,
With the fin'st the Silkeworme weaves
As finely woven; whose rich smell
The Ayre about thee so shall swell
That it shall have no power to moove.
A Ruffe of Pinkes thy Robe above
About thy necke so neatly set
That Art it cannot counterfet,
Which still shall looke so Fresh and new,
As if upon their Roots they grew:
And for thy head Ile have a Tyer
Of netting, made of Strawbery wyer,
And in each knot that doth compose
A Mesh, shall stick a halfe blowne Rose,
Red, damaske, white, in order set
About the sides, shall run a Fret
Of Primroses, the Tyer throughout
With Thrift and Dayses frindgd about;
All this faire Nimph Ile doe for thee,
So thou'lt leave him and goe with me.

CLEON - These be but weeds and Trash he brings,
Ile give thee solid, costly things,
His will wither and be gone
Before thou well canst put them on;
With Currall I will have thee Crown'd,
Whose Branches intricatly wound
Shall girt thy Temples every way;
And on the top of every Spray
Shall stick a Pearle orient and great,
Which so the wandring Birds shall cheat,
That some shall stoope to looke for Cheries,
As other for tralucent Berries.
And wondering, caught e'r they be ware
In the curld Tramels of thy hayre:
And for thy necke a Christall Chaine
Whose lincks shapt like to drops of Raine,
Vpon thy panting Breast depending,
Shall seeme as they were still descending,
And as thy breath doth come and goe,
So seeming still to ebbe and flow:
With Amber Bracelets cut like Bees,
Whose strange transparency who sees,
With Silke small as the Spiders Twist
Doubled so oft about thy Wrist,
Would surely thinke alive they were,

From Lillies gathering hony there.
Thy Buskins Ivory, caru'd like Shels
Of Scallope, which as little Bels
Made hollow, with the Ayre shall Chime,
And to thy steps shall keepe the time:
Leave Lalus, Lirope for me
And these shall thy rich dowry be.

LIROPE - Lalus for Flowers. Cleon for Iemmes,
For Garlands and for Diadems,
I shall be sped, why this is brave,
What Nimph can choicer Presents have,
With dressing, brading, frowncing, flowring,
All your jewels on me powring,
In this bravery being drest,
To the ground I shall be prest,
That I doubt the Nimphes will feare me,
Nor will venture to come neare me;
Never Lady of the May,
To this houre was halfe so gay;
All in flowers, all so sweet,
From the Crowne, beneath the Feet,
Amber, Currall, Ivory, Pearle,
If this cannot win a Gerle,
Ther's nothing can, and this ye wooe me,
Give me your hands and trust ye to me,
(Yet to tell ye I am loth)
That I'le have neither of you both;

LALUS - When thou shalt please to stem the flood,
(As thou art of the watry brood)
I'le have twelve Swannes more white than Snow,
Yokd for the purpose two and two,
To drawe thy Barge wrought of fine Reed
So well that it nought else shall need,
The Traces by which they shall hayle
Thy Barge; shall be the winding trayle
Of woodbynd; whose brave Tasseld Flowers
(The Sweetnesse of the Woodnimphs Bowres)
Shall be the Trappings to adorne,
The Swannes, by which thy Barge is borne,
Of flowred Flags I'le rob the banke
Of water-Cans and King-cups ranck
To be the Covering of thy Boate,
And on the Streame as thou do'st Floate,
The Naiades that haunt the deepe,
Themselves about thy Barge shall keepe,
Recording most delightfull Layes,

By Sea Gods written in thy prayse.
And in what place thou hapst to land,
There the gentle Siluery sand,
Shall soften, curled with the Aier
As sensible of thy repayre:
This my deare love I'le doe for thee,
So Thou't leave him and goe with me:

CLEON - Tush Nimphe his Swannes will prove but Geese,
His Barge drinke water like a Fleece;
A Boat is base, I'le thee provide,
A Chariot, wherein love may ride;
In which when bravely thou art borne,
Thou shalt looke like the gloryous morne
Ushering the Sunne, and such a one
As to this day was never none,
Of the Rarest Indian Gummes,
More pretious then your Balsamummes
Which I by Art have made so hard,
That they with Tooles may well be Carv'd
To make a Coach of: which shall be
Materyalls of this one for thee,
And of thy Chariot each small peece
Shall inlayd be with Amber Greece,
And guilded with the Yellow ore
Produc'd from Tagus wealthy shore;
In which along the pleasant Lawne,
With twelve white Stags thou shalt be drawne,
Whose brancht palmes of a stately height,
With severall nosegayes shall be dight;
And as thou ryd'st, thy Coach about,
For thy strong guard shall runne a Rout,
Of Estriges; whose Curled plumes,
Sen'sd with thy Chariots rich perfumes,
The scent into the Aier shall throw;
Whose naked Thyes shall grace the show;
Whilst the Woodnimphs and those bred
Vpon the mountayns, o'r thy head
Shall beare a Canopy of flowers,
Tinseld with drops of Aprill showers,
Which shall make more glorious showes
Then spangles, or your siluer Oas;
This bright nimph I'le doe for thee
So thou't leave him and goe with me.

LIROPE - Vie and reuie, like Chapmen profer'd,
Would't be receaved what you have offer'd;
Ye greater honour cannot doe me,

If not building Altars to me:
Both by Water and by Land,
Bardge and Chariot at command;
Swans upon the Streame to rawe me,
Stags upon the Land to drawe me,
In all this Pompe should I be seene,
What a pore thing were a Queene:
All delights in such excesse,
As but yee, who can expresse:
Thus mounted should the Nimphes me see,
All the troope would follow me,
Thinking by this state that I
Would asume a Deitie.
There be some in love have bin,
And I may commit that sinne,
And if e'r I be in love,
With one of you I feare twill prove,
But with which I cannot tell,
So my gallant Youths farewell.

THE THIRD NIMPHALL

DORON. NAIJS. CLORIS. CLAIA. DORILUS. CLOE. MERTILLA. FLORIMEL.

With Nimphes and Forresters.

Poetick Raptures, sacred fires,
With which Apollo his inspires,
This Nimphall gives you; and withall
Obserues the Muses Festivall.

Amongst th' Elizians many mirthfull Feasts,
At which the Muses are the certaine guests,
Th' obserue one Day with most Emperiall state,
To wise Apollo which they dedicate,
The Poets God; and to his Alters bring
Th' enamel'd Bravery of the beauteous spring,
And strew their Bowers with every precious sweet,
Which still wax fresh, most trod on with their feet;
With most choice flowers each Nimph doth brade her hayre,
And not the mean'st but bauldrick wise doth weare
Some goodly Garland, and the most renown'd
With curious Roseat Anadems are crown'd.
These being come into the place where they
Yearely obserue the Orgies to that day,
The Muses from their Heliconian spring

Their brimfull Mazers to the feasting bring:
When with deepe Draughts out of those plenteous Bowles,
The jocond Youth have swild their thirsty soules,
They fall enraged with a sacred heat,
And when their braines doe once begin to sweat
They into brave and Stately numbers breake,
And not a word that any one doth speake
But tis Prophetick, and so strangely farre
In their high fury they transported are,
As there's not one, on any thing can straine,
But by another answred is againe
In the same Rapture, which all sit to heare;
When as two Youths that soundly liquord were,
Dorilus and Doron, two as noble swayns
As ever kept on the Elizian playns,
First by their signes attention having woonne,
Thus they the Revels frolikly begunne.

DORON - Come Dorilus, let us be brave,
In lofty numbers let us rave,
With Rymes I will inrich thee.

DORILUS - Content say I, then bid the base,
Our wits shall runne the Wildgoosechase,
Spurre up, or I will swich thee.

DORON - The Sunne out of the East doth peepe,
And now the day begins to creepe,
Vpon the world at leasure.

DORILUS - The Ayre enamor'd of the Greaves,
The West winde stroaks the velvit leaves
And kisses them at pleasure.

DORON - The spinners webs twixt spray and spray,
The top of every bush make gay,
By filmy coards there dangling.

DORILUS - For now the last dayes evening dew
Euen to the full it selfe doth shew,
Each bough with Pearle bespangling.

DORON - O Boy how thy abundant vaine
Even like a Flood breaks from thy braine,
Nor can thy Muse be gaged.

DORILUS - Why nature forth did never bring
A man that like to me can sing,

If once I be enraged.

DORON - Why Dorilus I in my skill
Can make the swiftest Streame stand still,
Nay beare back to his springing.

DORILUS - And I into a Trance most deepe
Can cast the Birds that they shall sleepe
When fain'st they would be singing.

DORON - Why Dorilus thou mak'st me mad,
And now my wits begin to gad,
But sure I know not whither.

DORILUS - O Doron let me hug thee then,
There never was two madder men,
Then let us on together.

DORON - Hermes the winged Horse bestrid,
And thorow thick and thin he rid,
And floundred throw the Fountaine.

DORILUS - He spurd the Tit untill he bled,
So that at last he ran his head
Against the forked Mountaine,

DORON - How sayst thou, but pyde Iris got
Into great Iunos Chariot,
I spake with one that saw her.

DORILUS - And there the pert and sawcy Elfe,
Behau'd her as twere Iuno's selfe,
And made the Peacocks draw her.

DORON - Ile borrow Phœbus fiery Iades,
With which about the world he trades,
And put them in my Plow.

DORILUS - O thou most perfect frantique man,
Yet let thy rage be what it can,
Ile be as mad as thou.

DORON - Ile to great Iove, hap good, hap ill,
Though he with Thunder threat to kill,
And beg of him a boone.

DORILUS - To swerue up one of Cynthias beames,
And there to bath thee in the streames.

Discoverd in the Moone.

DORON - Come frolick Youth and follow me,
My frantique boy, and Ile show thee
The Countrey of the Fayries.

DORILUS - The fleshy Mandrake where't doth grow
In noonshade of the Mistletow,
And where the Phœnix Aryes.

DORON - Nay more, the Swallowes winter bed,
The Caverns where the Winds are bred,
Since thus thou talkst of showing.

DORILUS - And to those Indraughts Ile thee bring,
That wondrous and eternall spring
Whence th' Ocean hath its flowing.

DORON - We'll downe to the darke house of sleepe,
Where snoring Morpheus doth keepe,
And wake the drowsy Groome.

DORILUS - Downe shall the Dores and Windowes goe,
The Stooles upon the Floare we'll throw,
And roare about the Roome.

The Muses here commanded them to stay,
Commending much the caridge of their Lay
As greatly pleasd at this their madding Bout,
To heare how bravely they had borne it out
From first to the last, of which they were right glad,
By this they found that Helicon still had
That vertue it did anciently retaine
When Orpheus Lynus and th' Ascrean Swaine
Tooke lusty Rowses, which hath made their Rimes,
To last so long to all succeeding times.
And now amongst this beauteous Beautie here,
Two wanton Nimphes, though dainty ones they were,
Naijs and Cloe in their female fits
Longing to show the sharpnesse of their wits,
Of the nine Sisters speciall leave doe crave
That the next Bout they two might freely have,
Who having got the suffrages of all,
Thus to their Rimeing instantly they fall.

NAIJS - Amongst you all let us see
Who ist opposes mee,
Come on the proudest she

To answere my dittye.

CLOE - Why Naijs, that am I,
Who dares thy pride defie.
And that we soone shall try
Though thou be witty.

NAIJS - Cloe I scorne my Rime
Should obserue feet or time,
Now I fall, then I clime,
Where i'st I dare not.

CLOE - Give thy Invention wing,
And let her flert and fling,
Till downe the Rocks she ding,
For that I care not.

NAIJS - This presence delights me,
My freedome invites me,
The Season excytes me,
In Rime to be merry.

CLOE - And I beyond measure,
Am ravisht with pleasure,
To answer each Ceasure,
Untill thou beist weary.

NAIJS - Behold the Rosye Dawne,
Rises in Tinsild Lawne,
And smiling seemes to fawne,
Upon the mountaines.

CLOE - Awaked from her Dreames,
Shooting foorth goulden Beames
Dancing upon the Streames
Courting the Fountaines.

NAIJS - These more then sweet Showrets,
Intice up these Flowrets,
To trim up our Bowrets,
Perfuming our Coats.

CLOE - Whilst the Birds billing
Each one with his Dilling
The thickets still filling
With Amorous Noets.

NAIJS - The Bees up in hony rould,

More then their thighes can hould,
Lapt in their liquid gould,
Their Treasure us Bringing.

CLOE - To these Rillets purling
Upon the stones Curling,
And oft about wherling,
Dance tow'ard their springing.

NAIJS - The Wood-Nimphes sit singing,
Each Grove with notes ringing
Whilst fresh Ver is flinging
Her Bounties abroad.

CLOE - So much as the Turtle,
Upon the low Mertle,
To the meads fertle,
Her cares doth unload.

NAIJS - Nay 'tis a world to see,
In every bush and Tree,
The Birds with mirth and glee,
Woo'd as they woe.

CLOE - The Robin and the Wren,
Every Cocke with his Hen,
Why should not we and men,
Doe as they doe.

NAIJS - The Faires are hopping,
The small Flowers cropping,
And with dew dropping,
Skip thorow the Greaves.

CLOE - At Barly-breake they play
Merrily all the day,
At night themselves they lay
Upon the soft leaves.

NAIJS - The gentle winds sally,
Upon every Valley,
And many times dally
And wantonly sport.

CLOE - About the fields tracing,
Each other in chasing,
And often imbracing,
In amorous sort.

NAIJS - And Eccho oft doth tell
Wondrous things from her Cell,
As her what chance befell,
Learning to prattle.

CLOE - And now she sits and mocks
The Shepherds and their flocks,
And the Heards from the Rocks
Keeping their Cattle.

When to these Maids the Muses silence cry,
For 'twas the opinion of the Company,
That were not these two taken of, that they
Would in their Conflict wholly spend the day.
When as the Turne to Florimel next came,
A Nimph for Beauty of especiall name,
Yet was she not so lolly as the rest:
And though she were by her companions prest,
Yet she by no intreaty would be wrought
To sing, as by th' Elizian Lawes she ought:
When two bright Nimphes that her companions were,
And of all other onely held her deare,
Mild Claris and Mertilla, with faire speech
Their most beloved Florimel beseech,
T'obserue the Muses, and the more to wooe her,
They take their turnes, and thus they sing unto her.

CLORIS - Sing, Florimel, O sing, and wee
Our whole wealth will give to thee,
We'll rob the brim of every Fountaine,
Strip the sweets from every Mountaine,
We will sweepe the curled valleys,
Brush the bancks that mound our allyes,
We will muster natures dainties
When she wallowes in her plentyes,
The lushyous smell of every flower
New washt by an Aprill shower,
The Mistresse of her store we'll make thee
That she for her selfe shall take thee;
Can there be a dainty thing,
That's not thine if thou wilt sing.

MERTILLA - When the dew in May distilleth,
And the Earths rich bosome filleth,
And with Pearle embrouds each Meadow,
We will make them like a widow,
And in all their Beauties dresse thee,

And of all their spoiles possesse thee,
With all the bounties Zephyre brings,
Breathing on the yearely springs,
The gaudy bloomes of every Tree
In their most beauty when they be,
What is here that may delight thee,
Or to pleasure may excite thee,
Can there be a dainty thing
That's not thine if thou wilt sing.

But Florimel still sullenly replyes
I will not sing at all, let that suffice:
When as a Nimph one of the merry ging
Seeing she no way could be wonne to sing;
Come, come, quoth she, ye utterly undoe her
With your intreaties, and your reverence to her;
For praise nor prayers, she careth not a pin;
They that our froward Florimel would winne,
Must worke another way, let me come to her,
Either Ile make her sing, or Ile undoe her.

CLAIA - Florimel I thus coniure thee,
Since their gifts cannot alure thee;
By stampt Garlick, that doth stink
Worse then common Sewer, or Sink,
By Henbane, Dogsbane, Woolfsbane, sweet
As any Clownes or Carriers feet,
By stinging Nettles, pricking Teasels
Raysing blisters like the measels,
By the rough Burbreeding docks,
Rancker then the oldest Fox,
By filthy Hemblock, poysning more
Then any vlcer or old sore,
By the Cockle in the corne,
That smels farre worse then doth burnt horne,
By Hempe in water that hath layne,
By whose stench the Fish are slayne,
By Toadflax which your Nose may tast,
If you have a minde to cast,
May all filthy stinking Weeds
That e'r bore leafe, or e'r had seeds,
Florimel be given to thee,
If thou'lt not sing as well as wee.

At which the Nimphs to open laughter fell,
Amongst the rest the beauteous Florimel,
(Pleasd with the spell from Claia that came,
A mirthfull Gerle and given to sport and game)

As gamesome growes as any of them all,
And to this ditty instantly doth fall.

FLORIMEL - How in my thoughts should I contriue
The Image I am framing,
Which is so farre superlatiue,
As tis beyond all naming;
I would love of my counsell make,
And have his judgement in it,
But that I doubt he would mistake
How rightly to begin it,
It must be builded in the Ayre,
And tis my thoughts must doo it,
And onely they must be the stayre
From earth to mount me to it,
For of my Sex I frame my Lay,
Each houre, our selves forsaking,
How should I then finde out the way
To this my undertaking,
When our weake Fancies working still,
Yet changing every minnit,
Will shew that it requires some skill,
Such difficulty's in it.
We would things, yet we know not what,
And let our will be granted,
Yet instantly we finde in that
Something unthought of wanted:
Our joyes and hopes such shadowes are,
As with our motions varry,
Which when we oft have fetcht from farre,
With us they never tarry:
Some worldly crosse doth still attend,
What long we have in spinning,
And e'r we fully get the end
We lose of our beginning.
Our pollicies so peevish are,
That with themselves they wrangle,
And many times become the snare
That soonest us intangle;
For that the Love we beare our Friends
Though nere so strongly grounded,
Hath in it certaine oblique ends
If to the bottome sounded:
Our owne well wishing making it,
A pardonable Treason;
For that is deriv'd from witt,
And underpropt with reason.
For our Deare selves beloved sake

(Even in the depth of passion)
Our Center though our selves we make,
Yet is not that our station;
For whilst our Browes ambitious be
And youth at hand awayts us,
It is a pretty thing to see
How finely Beautie cheats us,
And whilst with tyme we tryfling stand
To practise Antique graces
Age with a pale and withered hand
Drawes Furowes in our faces.

When they which so desirous were before
To hear her sing; desirous are far more
To have her cease; and call to have her stayd
For she to much already had bewray'd.
And as the thrice three Sisters thus had grac'd
Their Celebration, and themselves had plac'd
Upon a Violet banck, in order all
Where they at will might view the Festifall
The Nimphs and all the lusty youth that were
At this brave Nimphall, by them honored there,
To Gratifie the heavenly Gerles againe
Lastly prepare in state to entertaine
Those sacred Sisters, fairely and confer,
On each of them, their prayse particular
And thus the Nimphes to the nine Muses sung.
When as the Youth and Forresters among
That well prepared for this businesse were,
Become the Chorus, and thus sung they there.

NIMPHES - Clio then first of those Celestiall nine
That daily offer to the sacred shryne,
Of wise Apollo; Queene of Stories,
Thou that vindicat'st the glories
Of passed ages, and renewst
Their acts which every day thou viewst,
And from a lethargy dost keepe
Old nodding time, else prone to sleepe.

CHORUS - Clio O crave of Phœbus to inspire
Vs, for his Altars with his holiest fire,
And let his glorious ever-shining Rayes
Give life and growth to our Elizian Bayes.

NIMPHES - Melpomine thou melancholly Maid
Next, to wise Phœbus we invoke thy ayd,
In Buskins that dost stride the Stage,

And in thy deepe distracted rage,
In blood-shed that dost take delight,
Thy obiect the most fearfull sight,
That lovest the sighes, the shreekes, and sounds
Of horrors, that arise from wounds.

CHORUS - Sad Muse, O crave of Phœbus to inspire
Vs for his Altars, with his holiest fire,
And let his glorious ever-shining Rayes
Give life and growth to our Elizian Bayes.

NIMPHES - Comick Thalia then we come to thee,
Thou mirthfull Mayden, onely that in glee
And loves deceits, thy pleasure tak'st,
Of which thy varying Scene that mak'st
And in thy nimble Sock do'st stirre
Loude laughter through the Theater,
That with the Peasant mak'st the sport,
As well as with the better sort.

CHORUS - Thalia crave of Phœbus to inspire
Vs for his Alters with his holyest fier;
And let his glorious ever-shining Rayes
Give life, and growth to our Elizian Bayes.

NIMPHES - Euterpe next to thee we will proceed,
That first sound'st out the Musick on the Reed,
With breath and fingers giv'ng life,
To the shrill Cornet and the Fyfe.
Teaching every stop and kaye,
To those upon the Pipe that playe,
Those which Wind-Instruments we call
Or soft, or lowd, or greate, or small,

CHORUS - Euterpe aske of Phebus to inspire,
Vs for his Alters with his holyest fire
And let his glorious ever-shining Rayes
Give life and growth to our Elizian Bayes.

NIMPHES - Terpsichore that of the Lute and Lyre,
And Instruments that sound with Cords and wyere,
That art the Mistres, to commaund
The touch of the most Curious hand,
When every Quaver doth Imbrace
His like in a true Diapase,
And every string his sound doth fill
Toucht with the Finger or the Quill.

CHORUS - Terpsichore, crave Phebus to inspire
Vs for his Alters with his holyest fier
And let his glorious ever-shining Rayes
Give life and growth to our Elizian Bayes.

NIMPHES - Then Erato wise muse on thee we call,
In Lynes to us that do'st demonstrate all,
Which neatly, with thy staffe and Bowe,
Do'st measure, and proportion showe;
Motion and Gesture that dost teach
That every height and depth canst reach,
And do'st demonstrate by thy Art
What nature else would not Impart.

CHORUS - Deare Erato crave Phebus to inspire
Vs for his Alters with his holyest fire,
And let his glorious ever-shining Rayes,
Give life and growth to our Elizian Bayes.

NIMPHES - To thee then brave Caliope we come
Thou that maintain'st, the Trumpet, and the Drum;
The neighing Steed that lovest to heare,
Clashing of Armes doth please thine eare,
In lofty Lines that do'st rehearse
Things worthy of a thundring verse,
And at no tyme are heard to straine,
On ought that suits a Common vayne.

CHORUS - Caliope, crave Phebus to inspire,
Vs for his Alters with his holyest fier,
And let his glorious ever-shining Rayes,
Give life and growth to our Elizian Bayes.

NIMPHES - Then Polyhymnia most delicious Mayd,
In Rhetoricks Flowers that art arayd,
In Tropes and Figures, richly drest,
The Fyled Phrase that lovest best,
That art all Elocution, and
The first that gav'st to understand
The force of wordes in order plac'd
And with a sweet deliuery grac'd.

CHORUS - Sweet Muse perswade our Phœbus to inspire
Vs for his Altars, with his holiest fire,
And let his glorious ever shining Rayes
Give life and growth to our Elizian Bayes.

NIMPHES - Lofty Vrania then we call to thee,

To whom the Heavens for ever opened be,
Thou th' Asterismes by name dost call,
And shewst when they doe rise and fall
Each Planets force, and dost divine
His working, seated in his Signe,
And how the starry Frame still roules
Betwixt the fixed stedfast Poles.

CHORUS - Urania aske of Phœbus to inspire
Vs for his Altars with his holiest fire,
And let his glorious ever-shining Rayes
Give life and growth to our Elizian Bayes.

THE FOURTH NIMPHALL

CLORIS and MERTILLA

Chaste Cloris doth disclose the shames
Of the Felician frantique Dames,
Mertilla striues t' apease her woe,
To golden wishes then they goe.

MERTILLA - Why how now Cloris, what, thy head
Bound with forsaken Willow?
Is the cold ground become thy bed?
The grasse become thy Pillow?
O let not those life-lightning eyes
In this sad vayle be shrowded,
Which into mourning puts the Skyes,
To see them over-clowded.

CLORIS - O my Mertilla doe not praise
These Lampes so dimly burning,
Such sad and sullen lights as these
Were onely made for mourning:
Their obiects are the barren Rocks
With aged Mosse o'r shaded;
Now whilst the Spring layes forth her Locks
With blossomes bravely braded.

MERTILLA - O Cloris, Can there be a Spring,
O my deare Nimph, there may not,
Wanting thine eyes it forth to bring,
Without which Nature cannot:
Say what it is that troubleth thee
Encrease by thy concealing,

Speake; sorrowes many times we see
Are lesned by revealing.

CLORIS - Being of late too vainely bent
And but at too much leisure;
Not with our Groves and Downes content,
But surfetting in pleasure;
Felicia's Fields I would goe see,
Where fame to me reported,
The choyce Nimphes of the world to be
From meaner beauties sorted;
Hoping that I from them might draw
Some graces to delight me,
But there such monstrous shapes I saw,
That to this houre affright me.
Throw the thick Hayre, that thatch'd their Browes,
Their eyes upon me stared,
Like to those raging frantique Froes
For Bacchus Feasts prepared:
Their Bodies, although straight by kinde,
Yet they so monstrous make them,
That for huge Bags blowne up with wind,
You very well may take them.
Their Bowels in their Elbowes are,
Whereon depend their Panches,
And their deformed Armes by farre
Made larger than their Hanches:
For their behauiour and their grace,
Which likewise should have priz'd them,
Their manners were as beastly base
As th' rags that so disguisd them;
All Anticks, all so impudent,
So fashon'd out of fashion,
As blacke Cocytus up had sent
Her Fry into this nation,
Whose monstrousnesse doth so perplex,
Of Reason and depriues me,
That for their sakes I loath my sex,
Which to this sadnesse driues me.

MERTILLA - O my deare Cloris be not sad,
Nor with these Furies danted,
But let these female fooles be mad,
With Hellish pride inchanted;
Let not thy noble thoughts descend
So low as their affections;
Whom neither counsell can amend,
Nor yet the Gods corrections:

Such mad folks ne'r let us bemoane,
But rather scorne their folly,
And since we two are here alone,
To banish melancholly,
Leave we this lowly creeping vayne
Not worthy admiration,
And in a brave and lofty strayne,
Lets exercise our passion,
With wishes of each others good,
From our abundant treasures,
And in this iocund sprightly mood:
Thus alter we our measures.

MERTILLA - O I could wish this place were strewd with Roses,
And that this Banck were thickly thrumd with Grasse
As soft as Sleave, or Sarcenet ever was,
Whereon my Cloris her sweet selfe reposes.

CLORIS - O that these Dewes Rosewater were for thee,
These Mists Perfumes that hang upon these thicks,
And that the Winds were all Aromaticks,
Which, if my wish could make them, they should bee.

MERTILLA - O that my Bottle one whole Diamond were,
So fild with Nectar that a Flye might sup,
And at one draught that thou mightst drinke it up,
Yet a Carouse not good enough I feare.

CLORIS - That all the Pearle, the Seas, or Indias have
Were well dissolv'd, and thereof made a Lake,
Thou there in bathing, and I by to take
Pleasure to see thee cleerer than the Wave.

MERTILLA - O that the Hornes of all the Heards we see,
Were of fine gold, or else that every horne
Were like to that one of the Vnicorne,
And of all these, not one but were thy Fee.

CLORIS - O that their Hooves were Iuory, or some thing,
Then the pur'st Iuory farre more Christalline,
Fild with the food wherewith the Gods doe dine,
To keepe thy Youth in a continuall Spring.

MERTILLA - O that the sweets of all the Flowers that grow,
The labouring ayre would gather into one,
In Gardens, Fields, nor Meadowes leaving none,
And all their Sweetnesse upon thee would throw.

CLORIS - Nay that those sweet harmonious straines we heare,
Amongst the lively Birds melodious Layes,
As they recording sit upon the Sprayes,
Were hovering still for Musick at thine eare.

MERTILLA - O that thy name were caru'd on every Tree,
That as these plants still great, and greater grow,
Thy name deare Nimph might be enlarged so,
That every Grove and Coppis might speake thee.

CLORIS - Nay would thy name upon their Rynds were set,
And by the Nimphes so oft and lowdly spoken,
As that the Ecchoes to that language broken
Thy happy name might hourely counterfet.

MERTILLA - O let the Spring still put sterne winter by,
And in rich Damaske let her Revell still,
As it should doe if I might have my will,
That thou mightst still walke on her Tapistry;
And thus since Fate no longer time alowes
Under this broad and shady Sicamore,
Where now we sit, as we have oft before;
Those yet unborne shall offer up their Vowes.

THE FIFTH NIMPHALL

CLAIA, LELIPA, CLARINAX a Hermit.

Of Garlands, Anadems, and Wreathes,
This Nimphall nought but sweetnesse breathes,
Presents you with delicious Posies,
And with powerfull Simples closes.

CLAIA - See where old Clarinax is set,
His sundry Simples sorting,
From whose experience we may get
What worthy is reporting.
Then Lelipa let us draw neere,
Whilst he his weedes is weathering,
I see some powerfull Simples there
That he hath late bin gathering.
Hail gentle Hermit, love thee speed,
And have thee in his keeping,
And ever helpe thee at thy need,
Be thou awake or sleeping.

CLARINAX - Ye payre of most Celestiall lights,
O Beauties three times burnisht,
Who could expect such heavenly wights
With Angels features furnisht;
What God doth guide you to this place,
To blesse my homely Bower?
It cannot be but this high grace
Proceeds from some high power;
The houres like hand-maids still attend,
Disposed at your pleasure,
Ordayned to noe other end
But to awaite your leasure;
The Deawes drawne up into the Aer,
And by your breathes perfumed,
In little Clouds doe hover there
As loath to be consumed:
The Aer moves not but as you please,
So much sweet Nimphes it owes you,
The winds doe cast them to their ease,
And amorously inclose you.

LELIPA - Be not too lauish of thy praise,
Thou good Elizian Hermit,
Lest some to heare such words as these,
Perhaps may flattery tearme it;
But of your Simples something say,
Which may discourse affoord us,
We know your knowledge lyes that way,
With subiects you have stor'd us.

CLAIA - We know for Physick yours you get,
Which thus you heere are sorting,
And upon garlands we are set,
With Wreathes and Posyes sporting:

LELIPA - The Chaplet and the Anadem,
The curled Tresses crowning,
We looser Nimphes delight in them,
Not in your Wreathes renowning.

CLARINAX - The Garland long agoe was worne,
As Time pleased to bestow it,
The Lawrell onely to adorne
The Conquerer and the Poet.
The Palme his due, who uncontrould,
On danger looking gravely,
When Fate had done the worst it could,
Who bore his Fortunes bravely.

Most worthy of the Oken Wreath
The Ancients him esteemed,
Who in a Battle had from death
Some man of worth redeemed.
About his temples Grasse they tye,
Himselfe that so behaved
In some strong Seedge by th' Enemy,
A City that hath saved.
A Wreath of Vervaine Herhauts weare,
Amongst our Garlands named,
Being sent that dreadfull newes to beare,
Offensiue warre proclaimed.
The Signe of Peace who first displayes,
The Oliue Wreath possesses:
The Lover with the Myrtle Sprayes
Adornes his crisped Tresses.
In Love the sad forsaken wight
The Willow Garland weareth:
The Funerall man befitting night,
The balefull Cipresse beareth.
To Pan we dedicate the Pine,
Whose Slips the Shepherd graceth:
Againe the Ivie and the Vine
On his, swolne Bacchus placeth.

CLAIA - The Boughes and Sprayes, of which you tell,
By you are rightly named,
But we with those of pretious smell
And colours are enflamed;
The noble Ancients to excite
Men to doe things worth crowning,
Not unperformed left a Rite,
To heighten their renowning:
But they that those rewards deuis'd,
And those brave wights that wore them
By these base times, though poorely priz'd,
Yet Hermit we adore them.
The store of every fruitfull Field
We Nimphes at will possessing,
From that variety they yeeld
Get flowers for every dressing:
Of which a Garland Ile compose,
Then busily attend me.
These flowers I for that purpose chose,
But where I misse amend me.

CLARINAX - Well Claia on with your intent,
Lets see how you will weave it,

Which done, here for a monument
I hope with me, you'll leave it.

CLAIA - Here Damaske Roses, white and red,
Out of my lap first take I,
Which still shall runne along the thred,
My chiefest Flower this make I:
Amongst these Roses in a row,
Next place I Pinks in plenty,
These double Daysyes then for show,
And will not this be dainty.
The pretty Pansy then Ile tye
Like Stones some Chaine inchasing,
And next to them their neere Alye,
The purple Violet placing.
The curious choyce, Clove Iuly-flower,
Whose kinds hight the Carnation
For sweetnesse of most soveraine power
Shall helpe my Wreath to fashion.
Whose sundry cullers of one kinde
First from one Root derived,
Them in their severall sutes Ile binde,
My Garland so contriued;
A course of Cowslips then I'll stick,
And here and there though sparely
The pleasant Primrose downe Ile prick
Like Pearles, which will show rarely:
Then with these Marygolds Ile make
My Garland somewhat swelling,
These Honysuckles then Ile take,
Whose sweets shall helpe their smelling:
The Lilly and the Flower delice,
For colour much contenting,
For that, I them doe only prize,
They are but pore in senting:
The Daffadill most dainty is
To match with these in meetnesse;
The Columbyne compar'd to this,
All much alike for sweetnesse.
These in their natures onely are
Fit to embosse the border,
Therefore Ile take especiall care
To place them in their order:
Sweet-Williams, Campions, Sops-in-Wine
One by another neatly:
Thus have I made this Wreath of mine,
And finished it featly.

LELIPA - Your Garland thus you finisht have,
Then as we have attended
Your leasure, likewise let me crave
I may the like be friended.
Those gaudy garish Flowers you chuse,
In which our Nimphes are flaunting,
Which they at Feasts and Brydals use,
The sight and smell inchanting:
A Chaplet me of Hearbs Ile make
Then which though yours be braver,
Yet this of myne I'le undertake
Shall not be short in fauour.
With Basill then I will begin,
Whose scent is wondrous pleasing,
This Eglantine I'le next put in,
The sense with sweetnes seasing.
Then in my Lavender I'le lay,
Muscado put among it,
And here and there a leafe of Bay,
Which still shall runne along it.
Germander, Marieram, and Tyme
Which used are for strewing,
With Hisop as an hearbe most pryme
Here in my wreath bestowing.
Then Balme and Mynt helps to make up
My Chaplet, and for Tryall,
Costmary that so likes the Cup,
And next it Penieryall
Then Burnet shall beare up with this
Whose leafe I greatly fansy,
Some Camomile doth not amisse,
With Sauory and some Tansy,
Then heere and there I'le put a sprig
Of Rosemary into it
Thus not too little or too big
Tis done if I can doe it.

CLARINAX - Claia your Garland is most gaye,
Compos'd of curious Flowers,
And so most lovely Lelipa,
This Chaplet is of yours,
In goodly Gardens yours you get
Where you your laps have laded;
My symples are by Nature set,
In Groves and Fields untraded.
Your Flowers most curiously you twyne,
Each one his place supplying.
But these rough harsher Hearbs of mine,

About me rudely lying,
Of which some dwarfish Weeds there be,
Some of a larger stature,
Some by experience as we see,
Whose names expresse their nature,
Heere is my Moly of much fame,
In Magicks often used,
Mugwort and Night-shade for the same
But not by me abused;
Here Henbane, Popy, Hemblock here,
Procuring Deadly sleeping,
Which I doe minister with Feare,
Not fit for each mans keeping.
Heere holy Veruayne, and heere Dill,
Against witchcraft much auailing.
Here Horhound gainst the Mad dogs ill
By biting, never failing.
Here Mandrake that procureth love,
In poysning philters mixed,
And makes the Barren fruitfull prove,
The Root about them fixed.
Inchaunting Lunary here lyes
In Sorceries excelling,
And this is Dictam, which we prize
Shot shafts and Darts expelling,
Here Saxifrage against the stone
That Powerfull is approved,
Here Dodder by whose helpe alone,
Ould Agues are removed
Here Mercury, here Helibore,
Ould Vlcers mundifying,
And Shepheards-Purse the Flux most sore,
That helpes by the applying;
Here wholsome Plantane, that the payne
Of Eyes and Eares appeases;
Here cooling Sorrell that againe
We use in hot diseases:
The medcinable Mallow here,
Asswaging sudaine Tumors,
The iagged Polypodium there,
To purge ould rotten humors,
Next these here Egremony is,
That helpes the Serpents byting,
The blessed Betony by this,
Whose cures deseruen writing:
This All-heale, and so nam'd of right,
New wounds so quickly healing,
A thousand more I could recyte,

Most worthy of Revealing,
But that I hindred am by Fate,
And busnesse doth prevent me,
To cure a mad man, which of late
Is from Felicia sent me.

CLAIA - Nay then thou hast inough to doe,
We pity thy enduring,
For they are there infected soe,
That they are past thy curing.

THE SIXTH NIMPHALL

SILVIUS, HALCIUS, MELANTHUS.

A Woodman, Fisher, and a Swaine
This Nimphall through with mirth maintaine,
Whose pleadings so the Nimphes doe please,
That presently they give them Bayes.

Cleere had the day bin from the dawne,
All chequerd was the Skye,
Thin Clouds like Scarfs of Cobweb Lawne
Vayld Heaven's most glorious eye.
The Winde had no more strength then this,
That leasurely it blew,
To make one leafe the next to kisse,
That closly by it grew.
The Rils that on the Pebbles playd,
Might now be heard at will;
This world they onely Musick made,
Else everything was still.
The Flowers like brave embraudred Gerles,
Lookt as they much desired,
To see whose head with orient Pearles,
Most curiously was tyred;
And to it selfe the subtle Ayre,
Such soverainty assumes,
That it receiu'd too large a share
From natures rich perfumes.
When the Elizian Youth were met,
That were of most account,
And to disport themselves were set
Vpon an easy Mount:
Neare which, of stately Firre and Pine
There grew abundant store,

The Tree that weepeth Turpentine,
And shady Sicamore.
Amongst this merry youthfull trayne
A Forrester they had,
A Fisher, and a Shepheards swayne
A liuely Countrey Lad:
Betwixt which three a question grew,
Who should the worthiest be,
Which violently they pursue,
Nor stickled would they be.
That it the Company doth please
This ciuill strife to stay,
Freely to heare what each of these
For his brave selfe could say:
When first this Forrester (of all)
That Silvius had to name,
To whom the Lot being cast doth fall,
Doth thus begin the Game.

SILVIUS - For my profession then, and for the life I lead,
All others to excell, thus for my selfe I plead;
I am the Prince of sports, the Forrest is my Fee,
He's not upon the Earth for pleasure liues like me;
The Morne no sooner puts her rosye Mantle on,
But from my quyet Lodge I instantly am gone,
When the melodious Birds from every Bush and Bryer,
Of the wilde spacious Wasts, make a continuall quire;
The motlied Meadowes then, new vernisht with the Sunne
Shute up their spicy sweets upon the winds that runne,
In easly ambling Gales, and softly seeme to pace,
That it the longer might their lushiousnesse imbrace:
I am clad in youthfull Greene, I other colour, scorne,
My silken Bauldrick beares my Beugle, or my Horne,
Which setting to my Lips, I winde so lowd and shrill,
As makes the Ecchoes showte from every neighbouring Hill:
My Doghooke at my Belt, to which my Lyam's tyde,
My Sheafe of Arrowes by, my Woodknife at my Syde,
My Crosse-bow in my Hand, my Gaffle or my Rack
To bend it when I please, or it I list to slack,
My Hound then in my Lyam, I by the Woodmans art
Forecast, where I may lodge the goodly Hie-palm'd Hart,
To viewe the grazing Heards, so sundry times I use,
Where by the loftiest Head I know my Deare to chuse,
And to unheard him then, I gallop o'r the ground
Vpon my wel-breath'd Nag, to cheere my earning Hound.
Sometime I pitch my Toyles the Deare aliue to take,
Sometime I like the Cry, the deep-mouth'd Kennell make,
Then underneath my Horse, I staulke my game to strike,

And with a single Dog to hunt him hurt, I like.
The Siluians are to me true subiects, I their King,
The stately Hart, his Hind doth to my presence bring,
The Buck his loved Doe, the Roe his tripping Mate,
Before me to my Bower, whereas I sit in State.
The Dryads, Hamadryads, the Satyres and the Fawnes
Oft play at Hyde and Seeke before me on the Lawnes,
The frisking Fayry oft when horned Cinthia shines
Before me as I walke dance wanton Matachynes,
The numerous feathered flocks that the wild Forrests haunt
Their Siluan songs to me, in cheerefull dittyes chaunte,
The Shades like ample Sheelds, defend me from the Sunne,
Through which me to refresh the gentle Riuelets runne,
No little bubling Brook from any Spring that falls
But on the Pebbles playes me pretty Madrigals.
I' th' morne I clime the Hills, where wholsome winds do blow,
At Noone-tyde to the Vales, and shady Groves below,
T'wards Euening I againe the Chrystall Floods frequent,
In pleasure thus my life continually is spent.
As Princes and great Lords have Pallaces, so I
Have in the Forrests here, my Hall and Gallery
The tall and stately Woods, which underneath are Plaine,
The Groves my Gardens are, the Heath and Downes againe
My wide and spacious walkes, then say all what ye can,
The Forrester is still your only gallant man.

He of his speech scarce made an end,
But him they load with prayse,
The Nimphes most highly him commend,
And vow to give him Bayes:
He's now cryde up of every one,
And who but onely he,
The Forrester's the man alone,
The worthyest of the three.
When some then th' other farre more stayd,
Wil'd them a while to pause,
For there was more yet to be sayd,
That might deserve applause,
When Halcius his turne next plyes,
And silence having wonne,
Roome for the fisher man he cryes,
And thus his Plea begunne.

HALCIUS - No Forrester, it so must not be borne away,
But heare what for himselfe the Fisher first can say,
The Chrystall current Streames continually I keepe,
Where every Pearle-pau'd Foard, and every Blew-eyd deepe
With me familiar are; when in my Boate being set,

My Oare I take in hand, my Augle and my Net
About me; like a Prince my selfe in state I steer,
Now up, now downe the Streame, now am I here, now ther,
The Pilot and the Fraught my selfe; and at my ease
Can land me where I list, or in what place I please,
The Siluer-scaled Sholes, about me in the Streames,
As thick as ye discerne the Atoms in the Beames,
Neare to the shady Banck where slender Sallowes grow,
And Willows their shag'd tops downe t'wards the waters bow
I shove in with my Boat to sheeld me from the heat,
Where chusing from my Bag, some prou'd especiall bayt,
The goodly well growne Trout I with my Angle strike,
And with my bearded Wyer I take the ravenous Pike,
Of whom when I have hould, he seldome breakes away
Though at my Lynes full length, soe long I let him play
Till by my hand I finde he well-nere wearyed be,
When softly by degrees I drawe him up to me.
The lusty Samon to, I oft with Angling take,
Which me above the rest most Lordly sport doth make,
Who feeling he is caught, such Frisks and bounds doth fetch,
And by his very strength my Line soe farre doth stretch,
As draws my floating Corcke downe to the very ground,
And wresting at my Rod, doth make my Boat turne round.
I never idle am, some tyme I bayt my Weeles,
With which by night I take the dainty siluer Eeles,
And with my Draughtnet then, I sweepe the streaming Flood,
And to my Tramell next, and Cast-net from the Mud,
I beate the Scaly brood, noe hower I idely spend,
But wearied with my worke I bring the day to end:
The Naijdes and Nymphes that in the Riuers keepe,
Which take into their care, the store of every deepe,
Amongst the Flowery flags, the Bullrushes and Reed,
That of the Spawne have charge (abundantly to breed)
Well mounted upon Swans, their naked bodys lend
To my discerning eye, and on my Boate attend,
And dance upon the Waves, before me (for my sake)
To th' Musick the soft wynd upon the Reeds doth make
And for my pleasure more, the rougher Gods of Seas
From Neptune's Court send in the blew Neriades,
Which from his bracky Realme upon the Billowes ride
And beare the Riuers backe with every streaming Tyde,
Those Billowes gainst my Boate, borne with delightfull Gales,
Oft seeming as I rowe to tell me pretty tales,
Whilst Ropes of liquid Pearle still load my laboring Oares,
As streacht upon the Streame they stryke me to the Shores:
The silent medowes seeme delighted with my Layes,
As sitting in my Boate I sing my Lasses praise,
Then let them that like, the Forrester up cry,

Your noble Fisher is your only man say I.

This speech of Halcius turn'd the Tyde,
And brought it so about,
That all upon the Fisher cryde,
That he would beare it out;
Him for the speech he made, to clap
Who lent him not a hand,
And said t'would be the Waters hap,
Quite to put downe the Land.
This while Melanthus silent sits,
(For so the Shepheard hight)
And having heard these dainty wits,
Each pleading for his right;
To heare them honor'd in this wise,
His patience doth prouoke,
When for a Shepheard roome he cryes,
And for himselfe thus spoke.

MELANTHUS - Well Fisher you have done, and Forrester for you
Your Tale is neatly tould, s'are both's to give you due,
And now my turne comes next, then heare a Shepherd speak:
My watchfulnesse and care gives day scarce leave to break,
But to the Fields I haste, my folded flock to see,
Where when I finde, nor Woolfe, nor Fox, hath iniur'd me,
I to my Bottle straight, and soundly baste my Throat,
Which done, some Country Song or Roundelay I roate
So merrily; that to the musick that I make,
I Force the Larke to sing ere she be well awake;
Then Baull my cut-tayld Curre and I begin to play,
He o'r my Shephooke leapes, now th'one, now th'other way,
Then on his hinder feet he doth himselfe aduance,
I tune, and to my note, my liuely Dog doth dance,
Then whistle in my Fist, my fellow Swaynes to call,
Downe goe our Hooks and Scrips, and we to Nine-holes fall,
At Dust-point, or at Quoyts, else are we at it hard,
All false and cheating Games, we Shepheards are debard;
Suruaying of my sheepe if Ewe or Wether looke
As though it were amisse, or with my Curre, or Crooke
I take it, and when once I finde what it doth ayle,
It hardly hath that hurt, but that my skill can heale;
And when my carefull eye, I cast upon my sheepe
I sort them in my Pens, and sorted soe I keepe:
Those that are bigst of Boane, I still reserue for breed,
My Cullings I put off, or for the Chapman feed.
When the Euening doth approach I to my Bagpipe take,
And to my Grazing flocks such Musick then I make,
That they forbeare to feed; then me a King you see,

I playing goe before, my Subiects followe me,
My Bell-weather most brave, before the rest doth stalke,
The Father of the flocke, and after him doth walke
My writhen-headed Ram, with Posyes crowned in pride
Fast to his crooked hornes with Rybands neatly ty'd
And at our Shepheards Board that's cut out of the ground,
My fellow Swaynes and I together at it round,
With Greencheese, clouted Cream, with Flawns, and Custards, stord,
Whig, Sider, and with Whey, I domineer a Lord,
When shering time is come I to the Riuer driue,
My goodly well-fleec'd Flocks: (by pleasure thus I thriue)
Which being washt at will; upon the shering day,
My wooll I foorth in Loaks, fit for the wynder lay,
Which upon lusty heapes into my Coate I heave,
That in the Handling feeles as soft as any Sleave,
When every Ewe two Lambes, that yeaned hath that yeare,
About her new shorne neck a Chaplet then doth weare;
My Tarboxe, and my Scrip, my Bagpipe, at my back,
My Sheephooke in my hand, what can I say I lacke;
He that a Scepter swayd, a sheephooke in his hand,
Hath not disdaind to have, for Shepheards then I stand;
Then Forester and you my Fisher cease your strife
I say your Shepheard leads your onely merry life,

They had not cryd the Forester,
And Fisher up before,
So much: but now the Nimphes preferre,
The Shephard ten tymes more,
And all the Ging goes on his side,
Their Minion him they make,
To him themselves they all apply'd,
And all his partie take;
Till some in their discretion cast,
Since first the strife begunne,
In all that from them there had past
None absolutly wonne;
That equall honour they should share;
And their deserts to showe,
For each a Garland they prepare,
Which they on them bestowe,
Of all the choisest flowers that weare,
Which purposly they gather,
With which they Crowne them, parting there,
As they came first together.

THE SEVENTH NIMPHALL

FLORIMEL, LELIPA, NAIJS, CODRUS a Feriman.

The Nimphes, the Queene of love pursue,
Which oft doth hide her from their view:
But lastly from th' Elizian Nation,
She banisht is by Proclamation.

FLORIMEL - Deare Lelipa, where hast thou bin so long,
Was't not enough for thee to doe me wrong;
To rob me of thy selfe, but with more spight
To take my Naijs from me, my delight?
Yee lazie Girles, your heads where have ye layd,
Whil'st Venus here her anticke prankes hath playd?

LELIPA - Nay Florimel, we should of you enquire,
The onely Mayden, whom we all admire
For Beauty, Wit, and Chastity, that you
Amongst the rest of all our Virgin crue,
In quest of her, that you so slacke should be,
And leave the charge to Naijs and to me.

FLORIMEL - Y'are much mistaken Lelipa, 'twas I,
Of all the Nimphes, that first did her descry,
At our great Hunting, when as in the Chase
Amongst the rest, me thought I saw one face
So exceeding faire, and curious, yet unknowne
That I that face not possibly could owne.
And in the course, so Goddesse like a gate,
Each step so full of maiesty and state;
That with my selfe, I thus resolu'd that she
Lesse then a Goddesse (surely) could not be:
Thus as Idalia, stedfastly I ey'd,
A little Nimphe that kept close by her side
I noted, as unknowne as was the other,
Which Cupid was disguis'd so by his mother.
The little purblinde Rogue, if you had seene,
You would have thought he verily had beene
One of Diana's Votaries so clad,
He every thing so like a Huntresse had:
And she had put false eyes into his head,
That very well he might us all have sped.
And still they kept together in the Reare,
But as the Boy should have shot at the Deare,
He shot amongst the Nimphes, which when I saw,
Closer up to them I began to draw;
And fell to hearken, when they naught suspecting,
Because I seem'd them utterly neglecting,

I heard her say, my little Cupid too't,
Now Boy or never, at the Beuie shoot,
Have at them Venus quoth the Boy anon,
I'le pierce the proud'st, had she a heart of stone:
With that I cryde out, Treason, Treason, when
The Nimphes that were before, turning agen
To understand the meaning of this cry,
They out of sight were vanish't presently.
Thus but for me, the Mother and the Sonne,
Here in Elizium, had us all undone.

NAIJS - Beleeve me, gentle Maide, 'twas very well,
But now heare me my beauteous Florimel,
Great Mars his Lemman being cryde out here,
She to Felicia goes, still to be neare
Th' Elizian Nimphes, for at us is her ayme,
The fond Felicians are her common game.
I upon pleasure idly wandring thither,
Something worth laughter from those fooles to gather,
Found her, who thus had lately beene surpriz'd,
Fearing the like, had her faire selfe disguis'd
Like an old Witch, and gave out to have skill
In telling Fortunes either good or ill;
And that more nearly she with them might close,
She cut the Cornes, of dainty Ladies Toes:
She gave them Phisicke, either to coole or moove them,
And powders too to make their sweet Hearts love them:
And her sonne Cupid, as her Zany went,
Carrying her boxes, whom she often sent
To know of her faire Patients how they slept.
By which meanes she, and the blinde Archer crept
Into their fauours, who would often Toy,
And tooke delight in sporting with the Boy;
Which many times amongst his waggish tricks,
These wanton Wenches in the bosome prickes;
That they before which had some franticke fits,
Were by his Witchcraft quite out of their wits.
Watching this Wisard, my minde gave me still
She some Impostor was, and that this skill
Was counterfeit, and had some other end.
For which discovery, as I did attend,
Her wrinckled vizard being very thin,
My piercing eye perceiu'd her cleerer skin
Through the thicke Riuels perfectly to shine;
When I perceiu'd a beauty so diuine,
As that so clouded, I began to pry
A little nearer, when I chanc't to spye
That pretty Mole upon her Cheeke, which when

I saw; suruaying every part agen,
Vpon her left hand, I perceiv'd the skarre
Which she receiued in the Troian warre;
Which when I found, I could not chuse but smile.
She, who againe had noted me the while,
And, by my carriage, found I had descry'd her,
Slipt out of sight, and presently doth hide her.

LELIPA - Nay then my dainty Girles, I make no doubt
But I my selfe as strangely found her out
As either of you both; in Field and Towne,
When like a Pedlar she went up and downe:
For she had got a pretty handsome Packe,
Which she had fardled neatly at her backe:
And opening it, she had the perfect cry,
Come my faire Girles, let's see, what will you buy.
Here be fine night Maskes, plastred well within,
To supple wrinckles, and to smooth the skin:
Heer's Christall, Corall, Bugle, Iet, in Beads,
Cornelian Bracelets for my dainty Maids:
Then Periwigs and Searcloth-Gloves doth show,
To make their hands as white as Swan or Snow:
Then takes she forth a curious gilded boxe,
Which was not opened but by double locks;
Takes them aside, and doth a Paper spred,
In which was painting both for white and red:
And next a piece of Silke, wherein there lyes
For the decay'd, false Breasts, false Teeth, false Eyes
And all the while shee's opening of her Packe,
Cupid with's wings bound close downe to his backe:
Playing the Tumbler on a Table gets,
And shewes the Ladies many pretty feats.
I seeing behinde him that he had such things,
For well I knew no boy but he had wings,
I view'd his Mothers beauty, which to me
Lesse then a Goddesse said, she could not be:
With that quoth I to her, this other day,
As you doe now, so one that came this way,
Shew'd me a neate piece, with the needle wrought,
How Mars and Venus were together caught
By polt-foot Vulcan in an Iron net;
It grieu'd me after that I chanc't to let,
It to goe from me: whereat waxing red,
Into her Hamper she hung downe her head,
As she had stoup't some noveltie to seeke,
But 'twas indeed to hide her blushing Cheeke:
When she her Trinkets trusseth up anon,
E'r we were 'ware, and instantly was gone.

FLORIMEL - But hearke you Nimphes, amongst our idle prate,
Tis current newes through the Elizian State,
That Venus and her Sonne were lately seene
Here in Elizium, whence they oft have beene
Banisht by our Edict, and yet still merry,
Were here in publique row'd o'r at the Ferry,
Where as 'tis said, the Ferryman and she
Had much discourse, she was so full of glee,
Codrus much wondring at the blind Boyes Bow.

NAIJS - And what it was, that easly you may know,
Codrus himselfe comes rowing here at hand.

LELIPA - Codrus Come hither, let your Whirry stand,
I hope upon you, ye will take no state
Because two Gods have grac't your Boat of late;
Good Ferry-man I pray thee let us heare
What talke ye had, aboard thee whilst they were.

CODRUS - Why thus faire Nimphes.
As I a Fare had lately past,
And thought that side to ply,
I heard one as it were in haste;
A Boate, a Boate, to cry,
Which as I was aboute to bring,
And came to view my Fraught,
Thought I; what more then heavenly thing,
Hath fortune hither brought.
She seeing mine eyes still on her were,
Soone, smilingly, quoth she;
Sirra, looke to your Roother there,
Why lookst thou thus at me?
And nimbly stept into my Boat,
With her a little Lad
Naked and blind, yet did I note,
That Bow and Shafts he had,
And two Wings to his Shoulders fixt,
Which stood like little Sayles,
With farre more various colours mixt,
Then be your Peacocks Tayles;
I seeing this little dapper Elfe,
Such Armes as these to beare,
Quoth I thus softly to my selfe,
What strange thing have we here,
I never saw the like thought I:
Tis more then strange to me,
To have a child have wings to fly,

And yet want eyes to see;
Sure this is some deuised toy,
Or it transform'd hath bin,
For such a thing, halfe Bird, halfe Boy,
I thinke was never seene;
And in my Boat I turnd about,
And wistly viewd the Lad,
And cleerely saw his eyes were out,
Though Bow and Shafts he had.
As wistly she did me behold,
How likst thou him, quoth she,
Why well, quoth I; and better should,
Had he but eyes to see.
How sayst thou honest friend, quoth she,
Wilt thou a Prentice take,
I thinke in time, though blind he be,
A Ferry-man hee'll make;
To guide my passage Boat quoth I,
His fine hands were not made,
He hath beene bred too wantonly
To undertake my trade;
Why helpe him to a Master then,
Quoth she, such Youths be scant,
It cannot be but there be men
That such a Boy do want.
Quoth I, when you your best have done,
No better way you'll finde,
Then to a Harper binde your Sonne,
Since most of them are blind.
The lovely Mother and the Boy,
Laught heartily thereat,
As at some nimble iest or toy,
To heare my homely Chat.
Quoth I, I pray you let me know,
Came he thus first to light,
Or by some sicknesse, hurt, or blow,
Depryued of his sight;
Nay sure, quoth she, he thus was borne,
Tis strange borne blind, quoth I,
I feare you put this as a scorne
On my simplicity;
Quoth she, thus blind I did him beare,
Quoth I, if't be no lye,
Then he 's the first blind man Ile sweare,
Ere practisd Archery,
A man, quoth she, nay there you misse,
He 's still a Boy as now,
Nor to be elder then he is,

The Gods will him alow;
To be no elder then he is,
Then sure he is some sprite
I straight replide, againe at this,
The Goddesse laught out right;
It is a mystery to me,
An Archer and yet blinde;
Quoth I againe, how can it be,
That he his marke should finde;
The Gods, quoth she, whose will it was
That he should want his sight,
That he in something should surpasse,
To recompence their spight,
Gave him this gift, though at his Game
He still shot in the darke,
That he should have so certaine ayme,
As not to misse his marke.
By this time we were come a shore,
When me my Fare she payd,
But not a word she uttered more,
Nor had I her bewrayd,
Of Venus nor of Cupid I
Before did never heare,
But that Fisher comming by
Then, told me who they were.

FLORIMEL - Well: against them then proceed
As before we have decreed,
That the Goddesse and her Child,
Be for ever hence exild,
Which Lelipa you shall proclaime
In our wise Apollo's name.

LELIPA - To all th' Elizian Nimphish Nation,
Thus we make our Proclamation,
Against Venus and her Sonne
For the mischeefe they have done,
After the next last of May,
The fixt and peremtory day,
If she or Cupid shall be found
Vpon our Elizian ground,
Our Edict, meere Rogues shall make them,
And as such, who ere shall take them,
Them shall into prison put,
Cupids wings shall then be cut,
His Bow broken, and his Arrowes
Given to Boyes to shoot at Sparrowes,
And this Vagabund be sent,

Hauing had due punishment
To mount Cytheron, which first fed him:
Where his wanton Mother bred him,
And there out of her protection
Dayly to receiue correction;
Then her Pasport shall be made,
And to Cyprus Isle conuayd,
And at Paphos in her Shryne,
Where she hath been held diuine,
For her offences found contrite,
There to liue an Anchorite.

THE EIGHTH NIMPHALL

MERTILLA, CLAIA, CLORIS.

A Nimph is marryed to a Fay,
Great preparations for the Day,
All Rites of Nuptials they recite you
To the Brydall and inuite you.

MERTILLA - But will our Tita wed this Fay?

CLAIA - Yea, and to morrow is the day.

MERTILLA - But why should she bestow her selfe
Vpon this dwarfish Fayry Elfe?

CLAIA - Why by her smalnesse you may finde,
That she is of the Fayry kinde,
And therefore apt to chuse her make
Whence she did her begining take:
Besides he 's deft and wondrous Ayrye,
And of the noblest of the Fayry,
Chiefe of the Crickets of much fame,
In Fayry a most ancient name.
But to be briefe, 'tis cleerely done,
The pretty wench is woo'd and wonne.

CLORIS - If this be so, let us prouide
The Ornaments to fit our Bryde.
For they knowing she doth come
From us in Elizium,
Queene Mab will looke she should be drest
In those attyres we thinke our best,
Therefore some curious things lets give her,

E'r to her Spouse we her deliuer.

MERTILLA - Ile have a Iewell for her eare,
(Which for my sake Ile have her weare)
'T shall be a Dewdrop, and therein
Of Cupids I will have a twinne,
Which strugling, with their wings shall break
The Bubble, out of which shall leak,
So sweet a liquor as shall move
Each thing that smels, to be in love.

CLAIA - Beleeve me Gerle, this will be fine,
And to this Pendant, then take mine;
A Cup in fashion of a Fly,
Of the Linxes piercing eye,
Wherein there sticks a Sunny Ray
Shot in through the cleerest day,
Whose brightnesse Venus selfe did move,
Therein to put her drinke of Love,
Which for more strength she did distill,
The Limbeck was a Phœnix quill,
At this Cups delicious brinke,
A Fly approching but to drinke,
Like Amber or some precious Gumme
It transparant doth become.

CLORIS - For Iewels for her eares she's sped,
But for a dressing for her head
I thinke for her I have a Tyer,
That all Fayryes shall admyre,
The yellowes in the full-blowne Rose,
Which in the top it doth inclose
Like drops of gold Oare shall be hung;
Vpon her Tresses, and among
Those scattered seeds (the eye to please)
The wings of the Cantharides:
With some o' th' Raine-bow that doth raile
Those Moons in, in the Peacocks taile:
Whose dainty colours being mixt
With th' other beauties, and so fixt,
Her lovely Tresses shall appeare,
As though upon a flame they were.
And to be sure she shall be gay,
We'll take those feathers from the Iay;
About her eyes in Circlets set,
To be our Tita's Coronet.

MERTILLA - Then dainty Girles I make no doubt,

But we shall neatly send her out:
But let's amongst our selves agree,
Of what her wedding Gowne shall be.

CLAIA - Of Pansie, Pincke, and Primrose leaves,
Most curiously laid on in Threaves:
And all embroydery to supply,
Powthred with flowers of Rosemary:
A trayle about the skirt shall runne,
The Silkewormes finest, newly spunne;
And every Seame the Nimphs shall sew
With th' smallest of the Spinners Clue:
And having done their worke, againe
These to the Church shall beare her Traine:
Which for our Tita we will make
Of the cast slough of a Snake,
Which quiuering as the winde doth blow,
The Sunne shall it like Tinsell shew.

CLORIS - And being led to meet her mate,
To make sure that she want no state,
Moones from the Peacockes tayle wee'll shred,
With feathers from the Pheasants head:
Mix'd with the plume of (so high price,)
The precious bird of Paradice.
Which to make up, our Nimphes shall ply
Into a curious Canopy.
Borne o're her head (by our enquiry)
By Elfes, the fittest of the Faery.

MERTILLA - But all this while we have forgot
Her Buskins, neighbours, have we not?

CLAIA - We had, for those I'le fit her now,
They shall be of the Lady-Cow:
The dainty shell upon her backe
Of Crimson strew'd with spots of blacke;
Which as she holds a stately pace,
Her Leg will wonderfully grace.

CLORIS - But then for musicke of the best,
This must be thought on for the Feast.

MERTILLA - The Nightingale of birds most choyce,
To doe her best shall straine her voyce;
And to this bird to make a Set,
The Mauis, Merle, and Robinet;
The Larke, the Lennet, and the Thrush,

That make a Quier of every Bush.
But for still musicke, we will keepe
The Wren, and Titmouse, which to sleepe
Shall sing the Bride, when shee's alone
The rest into their chambers gone.
And like those upon Ropes that walke
On Gossimer, from staulke to staulke,
The tripping Fayry tricks shall play
The evening of the wedding day.

CLAIA - But for the Bride-bed, what were fit,
That hath not beene talk'd of yet.

CLORIS - Of leaves of Roses white and red,
Shall be the Covering of her bed:
The Curtaines, Valence, Tester, all,
Shall be the flower Imperiall,
And for the Fringe, it all along
With azure Harebels shall be hung:
Of Lillies shall the Pillowes be,
With downe stuft of the Butterflee.

MERTILLA - Thus farre we handsomely have gone,
Now for our Prothalamion
Or Marriage song of all the rest,
A thing that much must grace our feast.
Let us practise then to sing it,
Ere we before th' assembly bring it:
We in Dialogues must doe it,
The my dainty Girles set to it.

CLAIA - This day must Tita marryed be,
Come Nimphs this nuptiall let us see.

MERTILLA - But is it certaine that ye say,
Will she wed the Noble Faye?

CLORIS - Sprinckle the dainty flowers with dewes,
Such as the Gods at Banquets use:
Let Hearbs and Weeds turne all to Roses,
And make proud the posts with posies:
Shute your sweets into the ayre,
Charge the morning to be fayre.

CLAIA   } For our Tita is this day,
MERTILLA } To be married to a Faye.

CLAIA - By whom then shall our Bride be led

To the Temple to be wed.

MERTILLA - Onely by your selfe and I,
Who that roomth should else supply?

CLORIS - Come bright Girles, come altogether,
And bring all your offrings hither,
Ye most brave and Buxome Beuye,
All your goodly graces Leuye,
Come in Maiestie and state
Our Brydall here to celebrate.

MERTILLA } For our Tita is this day,
CLAIA   } Married to a noble Faye.

CLAIA - Whose lot wilt be the way to strow
On which to Church our Bride must goe?

MERTILLA - That I think as fit'st of all,
To lively Lelipa will fall.

CLORIS - Summon all the sweets that are,
To this nuptiall to repayre;
Till with their throngs themselves they smother,
Strongly styfling one another;
And at last they all consume,
And vanish in one rich perfume.

MERTILLA } For our Tita is this day,
CLAIA   } Married to a noble Faye.

MERTILLA - By whom must Tita married be,
'Tis fit we all to that should see?

CLAIA - The Priest he purposely doth come,
Th' Arch Flamyne of Elizium.

CLORIS - With Tapers let the Temples shine,
Sing to Himen, Hymnes diuine:
Load the Altars till there rise
Clouds from the burnt sacrifice;
With your Sensors fling aloofe
Their smels, till they ascend the Roofe.

MERTILLA } For our Tita is this day,
CLAIA   } Married to a noble Fay.

MERTILLA - But comming backe when she is wed,

Who breakes the Cake above her head.

CLAIA - That shall Mertilla, for shee's tallest,
And our Tita is the smallest.

CLORIS - Violins, strike up aloud,
Ply the Gitterne, scowre the Crowd,
Let the nimble hand belabour
The whistling Pipe, and drumbling Taber:
To the full the Bagpipe racke,
Till the swelling leather cracke.

MERTILLA } For our Tita is this day,
CLAIA   } Married to a noble Fay.

CLAIA - But when to dyne she takes her seate
What shall be our Tita's meate?

MERTILLA - The Gods this Feast, as to begin,
Have sent of their Ambrosia in.

CLORIS - Then serue we up the strawes rich berry,
The Respas, and Elizian Cherry:
The virgin honey from the flowers
In Hibla, wrought in Flora's bowers:
Full Bowles of Nectar, and no Girle
Carouse but in dissolued Pearle.

MERTILLA } For our Tita is this day,
CLAIA   } Married to a noble Fay.

CLAIA - But when night comes, and she must goe
To Bed, deare Nimphes what must we doe?

MERTILLA - In the Posset must be brought,
And Poynts be from the Bridegroome caught.

CLORIS - In Maskes, in Dances, and delight,
And reare Banquets spend the night:
Then about the Roome we ramble,
Scatter Nuts, and for them scramble:
Ouer Stooles, and Tables tumble,
Never thinke of noyse nor rumble.

MERTILLA } For our Tita is this day,
CLAIA   } Married to a noble Fay.

MUSES and NIMPHS.

The Muses spend their lofty layes,
Vpon Apollo and his prayse;
The Nimphs with Gems his Alter build,
This Nimphall is with Phœbus fild.

A Temple of exceeding state,
The Nimphes and Muses rearing,
Which they to Phœbus dedicate,
Elizium ever cheering:
These Muses, and those Nimphes contend
This Phane to Phœbus offring,
Which side the other should transcend,
These praise, those prizes proffering,
And at this long appointed day,
Each one their largesse bringing,
Those nine faire Sisters led the way
Thus to Apollo singing.

THE MUSES - Thou youthfull God that guid'st the howres,
The Muses thus implore thee,
By all those Names, due to thy powers,
By which we still adore thee.
Sol, Tytan, Delius, Cynthius, styles
Much reverence that have wonne thee,
Deriu'd from Mountaines as from Iles
Where worship first was done thee.
Rich Delos brought thee forth diuine,
Thy Mother thither driven,
At Delphos thy most sacred shrine,
Thy Oracles were given.
In thy swift course from East to West,
They minutes misse to finde thee,
That bear'st the morning on thy breast,
And leau'st the night behinde thee.
Vp to Olimpus top so steepe,
Thy startling Coursers currying;
Thence downe to Neptunes vasty deepe,
Thy flaming Charriot hurrying.
Eos, Ethon, Phlegon, Pirois, proud,
Their lightning Maynes advancing:
Breathing forth fire on every cloud
Upon their journey prancing.
Whose sparkling hoofes, with gold for speed

Are shod, to scape all dangers,
Where they vpon Ambrosia feed,
In their celestiall Mangers.
Bright Colatina, that of hils
Is Goddesse, and hath keeping
Her Nimphes, the cleere Oreades wils
Tattend theefrom thy sleeping.
Great Demogorgon feeles thy might,
His Mynes about him heating:
Who through his bosome dart'st thy light,
Within the Center sweating.
If thou but touch thy golden Lyre,
Thou Minos mov'st to heare thee:
The Rockes feele in themselves a fire,
And rise up to come neere thee.
'Tis thou that Physicke didst devise
Hearbs by their natures calling:
Of which some opening at thy Rise,
And closing at thy falling.
Fayre Hyacinth thy most lou'd Lad,
That with the sledge thou sluest;
Hath in a flower the life he had,
Whose root thou still renewest,
Thy Daphne thy beloued Tree,
That scornes thy Fathers Thunder,
And thy deare Clitia yet we see,
Not time from thee can sunder;
From thy bright Bow that Arrow flew
(Snatcht from thy golden Quiuer)
Which that fell Serpent Python slew,
Renowning thee for ever.
The Actian and the Pythian Games
Deuised were to praise thee,
With all th' Apolinary names
That th' Ancients thought could raise thee.
A Shryne vpon this Mountaine his,
To thee we'll haue erected,
Which thou the God of Poesie
Must care to haue protected:
With thy lov'd Cinthus that shall share,
With all his shady Bowers,
Nor Licia's Cragus shall compare
With this, for thee, of ours.
Thus having sung, the Nimphish Crue
Thrust in amongst them thronging,
Desiring they might have the due
That was to them belonging.
Quoth they, ye Muses as diuine,

Are in his glories graced,
But it is we must build the Shryne
Wherein they must be placed;
Which of those precious Gemmes we'll make
That Nature can affoord us,
Which from that plenty we will take,
Wherewith we here have stor'd us:
O glorious Phœbus most diuine,
Thine Altars then we hallow.
And with those stones we build a Shryne
To thee our wise Apollo.

THE NIMPHES - No Gem, from Rocke, Seas, running streames,
(Their numbers let us muster)
But hath from thy most powerfull beames
The Vertue and the Lustre;
The Diamond, the King of Gemmes,
The first is to be placed,
That glory is of Diadems,
Them gracing, by them graced:
In whom thy power the most is seene,
The raging fire refelling:
The Emerauld then, most deepely greene,
For beauty most excelling,
Resisting poyson often prou'd
By those about that beare it.
The cheerfull Ruby then, much lou'd,
That doth reuiue the spirit,
Whose kinde to large extensure growne
The colour so enflamed,
Is that admired mighty stone
The Carbunckle that's named,
Which from it such a flaming light
And radiency eiecteth,
That in the very dark'st of night
The eye to it directeth.
The yellow Iacynth, strengthening Sense,
Of which who hath the keeping,
No Thunder hurts nor Pestilence,
And much prouoketh sleeping:
The Chrisolite, that doth resist
Thirst, proved, never failing,
The purple colored Amatist,
'Gainst strength of wine prevailing;
The verdant gay greene Smaragdus,
Most soveraine over passion:
The Sardonix approu'd by us
To master Incantation.

Then that celestiall colored stone
The Saphyre, heavenly wholly,
Which worne, there wearinesse is none,
And cureth melancholly:
The Lazulus, whose pleasant blew
With golden vaines is graced;
The Iaspis, of so various hew,
Amongst our other placed;
The Onix from the Ancients brought,
Of wondrous Estimation,
Shall in amongst the rest be wrought
Our sacred Shryne to fashion;
The Topas, we'll stick here and there,
And sea-greene colored Berill,
And Turkesse, which who haps to beare
Is often kept from perill,
To Selenite, of Cynthia's light,
So nam'd, with her still ranging,
Which as she wanes or waxeth bright
Its colours so are changing.
With Opalls, more then any one,
We'll deck thine Altar fuller,
For that of every precious stone,
It doth retaine some colour;
With bunches of Pearle Paragon
Thine Altars underpropping,
Whose base is the Cornelian,
Strong bleeding often stopping:
With th' Agot, very oft that is
Cut strangely in the Quarry,
As Nature ment to show in this,
How she her selfe can varry:
With worlds of Gems from Mines and Seas
Elizium well might store us:
But we content our selves with these
That readiest lye before us:
And thus O Phœbus most diuine
Thine Altars still we hallow,
And to thy Godhead reare this Shryne
Our onely wise Apollo.

THE TENTH NIMPHALL

NAIIS, CLAIA, CORBILUS, SATYRE.

A Satyre on Elizium lights,

Whose vgly shape the Nimphes affrights,
Yet when they heare his iust complaint,
They make him an Elizian Saint.

CORBILUS - What; breathles Nimphs? bright Virgins let me know
What suddaine cause constraines ye to this haste?
What have ye seene that should affright ye so?
What might it be from which ye flye so fast?
I see your faces full of pallid feare,
As though some perill followed on your flight;
Take breath a while, and quickly let me heare
Into what danger ye have lately light.

NAIJS - Never were poore distressed Gerles so glad,
As when kinde, loved Corbilus we saw,
When our much haste us so much weakned had,
That scarcely we our wearied breathes could draw,
In this next Grove under an aged Tree,
So fell a monster lying there we found,
As till this day, our eyes did never see,
Nor ever came on the Elizian ground.
Halfe man, halfe Goate, he seem'd to us in show,
His upper parts our humane shape doth beare,
But he's a very perfect Goat below,
His crooked Cambrils arm'd with hoofe and hayre.

CLAIA - Through his leane Chops a chattering he doth make
Which stirres his staring beastly driueld Beard,
And his sharpe hornes he seem'd at us to shake,
Canst thou then blame us though we are afeard.

CORBILUS - Surely it seemes some Satyre this should be,
Come and goe back and guide me to the place,
Be not affraid, ye are safe enough with me,
Silly and harmlesse be their Siluan Race.

CLAIA - How Corbilus; a Satyre doe you say?
How should he over high Parnassus hit?
Since to these fields there's none can finde the way,
But onely those the Muses will permit.

CORBILUS - 'Tis true; but oft, the sacred Sisters grace
The silly Satyre, by whose plainnesse, they
Are taught the worlds enormities to trace,
By beastly mens abhominable way;
Besyde he may be banisht his owne home
By this base time, or be so much distrest,
That he the craggy by-clift Hill hath clome

To finde out these more pleasant Fields of rest.

NAIJS - Yonder he sits, and seemes himselfe to bow
At our approach, what doth our presence awe him?
Me thinks he seemes not halfe so vgly now,
As at the first, when I and Claia saw him.

CORBILUS - 'Tis an old Satyre, Nimph, I now discerne,
Sadly he sits, as he were sick or lame,
His lookes would say, that we may easly learne
How, and from whence, he to Elizium came.
Satyre, these Fields, how cam'st thou first to finde?
What Fate first show'd thee this most happy store?
When never any of thy Siluan kinde
Set foot on the Elizian earth before?

SATYRE - O never aske, how I came to this place,
What cannot strong necessity finde out?
Rather bemoane my miserable case,
Constrain'd to wander this wide world about:
With wild Silvanus and his woody crue,
In Forrests I, at liberty and free,
Liu'd in such pleasure as the world ne'r knew,
Nor any rightly can conceiue but we.
This iocond life we many a day enioy'd,
Till this last age, those beastly men forth brought,
That all those great and goodly Woods destroy'd.
Whose growth their Grandsyres, with such sufferance sought,
That faire Felicia which was but of late,
Earth's Paradice, that never had her Peere,
Stands now in that most lamentable state,
That not a Siluan will inhabit there;
Where in the soft and most delicious shade,
In heat of Summer we were wont to play,
When the long day too short for us we made,
The slyding houres so slyly stole away;
By Cynthia's light, and on the pleasant Lawne,
The wanton Fayry we were wont to chase,
Which to the nimble cloven-footed Fawne,
Vpon the plaine durst boldly bid the base.
The sportiue Nimphes, with shouts and laughter shooke
The Hils and Valleyes in their wanton play,
Waking the Ecchoes, their last words that tooke,
Till at the last, they lowder were then they.
The lofty hie Wood, and the lower spring,
Sheltring the Deare, in many a suddaine shower;
Where Quires of Birds, oft wonted were to sing,
The flaming Furnace wholly doth deuoure;

Once faire Felicia, but now quite defac'd,
Those Braveries gone wherein she did abound,
With dainty Groves, when she was highly grac'd
With goodly Oake, Ashe, Elme, and Beeches croun'd:
But that from heaven their judgement blinded is,
In humane Reason it could never be,
But that they might have cleerly seene by this,
Those plagues their next posterity shall see.
The little Infant on the mothers Lap
For want of fire shall be so sore distrest,
That whilst it drawes the lanke and empty Pap,
The tender lips shall freese unto the breast;
The quaking Cattle which their Warmstall want,
And with bleake winters Northerne winde opprest,
Their Browse and Stover waxing thin and scant,
The hungry Groves shall with their Caryon feast.
Men wanting Timber wherewith they should build,
And not a Forrest in Felicia found,
Shall be enforc'd upon the open Field,
To dig them caves for houses in the ground:
The Land thus rob'd, of all her rich Attyre,
Naked and bare her selfe to heaven doth show,
Begging from thence that love would dart his fire
Vpon those wretches that disrob'd her so;
This beastly Brood by no meanes may abide
The name of their brave Ancestors to heare,
By whom their sordid slavery is descry'd,
So unlike them as though not theirs they were,
Nor yet they sense, nor understanding have,
Of those brave Muses that their Country song,
But with false Lips ignobly doe deprave
The right and honour that to them belong;
This cruell kinde thus Viper-like deuoure
That fruitfull soyle which them too fully fed;
The earth doth curse the Age, and every houre
Againe, that it these viprous monsters bred.
I seeing the plagues that shortly are to come
Vpon this people cleerely them forsooke:
And thus am light into Elizium,
To whose straite search I wholly me betooke.

NAIIS - Poore silly creature, come along with us,
Thou shalt be free of the Elizian fields:
Be not dismaid, nor inly grieved thus,
This place content in all abundance yeelds.
We to the cheerefull presence will thee bring,
Of loves deare Daughters, where in shades they sit,
Where thou shalt heare those sacred Sisters sing,

Most heavenly Hymnes, the strength and life of wit:

CLAIA - Where to the Delphian God upon their Lyres
His Priests seeme rauisht in his height of praise:
Whilst he is crowning his harmonious Quiers
With circling Garlands of immortall Bayes.

CORBILUS - Here liue in blisse, till thou shalt see those slaues,
Who thus set vertue and desert at nought:
Some sacrific'd upon their Grandsires graves,
And some like beasts in markets sold and bought.
Of fooles and madmen leave thou then the care,
That have no understanding of their state:
For whom high heaven doth so iust plagues prepare,
That they to pitty shall conuert thy hate.
And to Elizium be thou welcome then,
Vntill those base Felicians thou shalt heare,
By that vile nation captiued againe,
That many a glorious age their captiues were.

Michael Drayton – A Short Biography by Cyril Brett

Michael Drayton was born in 1563, at Hartshill, near Atherstone, in Warwickshire.

He became a page to Sir Henry Goodere, at Polesworth Hall: his own words give the best picture of his early years here. His education would seem to have been good, but ordinary; and it is very doubtful if he ever went to a university. Besides the authors mentioned in the Epistle to Henry Reynolds, he was certainly familiar with Ovid and Horace, and possibly with Catullus: while there seems no reason to doubt that he read Greek, though it is quite true that his references to Greek authors do not prove any first-hand acquaintance. He understood French, and read Rabelais and the French sonneteers, and he seems to have been acquainted with Italian. His knowledge of English literature was wide, and his judgement good: but his chief bent lay towards the history, legendary and otherwise, of his native country, and his vast stores of learning on this subject bore fruit in the Poly-Olbion.

While still at Polesworth, Drayton fell in love with his patron's younger daughter, Anne; and, though she married, in 1596, Sir Henry Raynsford of Clifford, Drayton continued his devotion to her for many years, and also became an intimate friend of her husband's, writing a sincere elegy on his death.

About February, 1591, Drayton paid a visit to London, and published his first work, the Harmony of the Church, a series of paraphrases from the Old Testament, in fourteen-syllabled verse of no particular vigour or grace. This book was immediately suppressed by order of Archbishop Whitgift, possibly because it was supposed to savour of Puritanism. The author, however, published another edition in 1610; indeed, he seems to have had a fondness for this style of work; for in 1604 he published a dull poem, Moyses in a Map of his Miracles, re-issued in 1630 as Moses his Birth and Miracles. Accompanying this piece, in 1630, were two other 'Divine poems': Noah's Floud, and David and Goliath. Noah's Floud is, in part, one of Drayton's happiest attempts at the catalogue style of bestiary; and Mr. Elton finds in it some foreshadowing of the manner of Paradise Lost. But, as a whole, Drayton's attempts in this direction deserve the oblivion into which they, in common with the similar productions of other authors, have fallen. In the dedication and preface to the Harmony of the Church are some of the few traces of Euphuism shown in Drayton's work; passages in the Heroical Epistles also occur to the mind He was always averse to affectation, literary or otherwise, and in Elegy VIII deliberately condemns Lyly's fantastic style.

Probably before Drayton went up to London, Sir Henry Goodere saw that he would stand in need of a patron more powerful than the master of Polesworth, and introduced him to the Earl and Countess of Bedford. Those who believe Drayton to have been a Pope in petty spite, identify the 'Idea' of his earlier poems with Lucy, Countess of Bedford; though they are forced to acknowledge as self-evident that the 'Idea' of his later work is Anne, Lady Raynsford. They then proceed to say that Drayton, after consistently honouring the Countess in his verse for twelve years, abruptly transferred his allegiance, not forgetting to heap foul abuse on his former patroness, out of pique at some temporary withdrawal of favour. Not only is this directly contrary to all we know and can infer of Drayton's character, but Mr. Elton has decisively disproved it by a summary of bibliographical and other evidence. Into the question it is here unnecessary to enter, and it has been mentioned only because it alone, of the many Drayton-controversies, has cast any slur on the poet's reputation.

In 1593, Drayton published Idea, the Shepherds Garland, in nine Eclogues; in 1606 he added a tenth, the best of all, to the new edition, and rearranged the order, so that the new eclogue became the ninth. In these Pastorals, while following the Shepherds Calendar in many ways, he already displays something of the sturdy independence which characterized him through life. He abandons Spenser's quasi-rustic dialect, and, while keeping to most of the pastoral conventions, such as the singing-match and threnody, he contrives to introduce something of a more natural and homely strain. He keeps the political allusions, notably in the Eclogue containing the song in praise of Beta, who is, of course, Queen Elizabeth. But an over-bold remark in the last line of that song was struck out in 1606; and the new eclogue has no political reference. He is not ashamed to allude directly to Spenser; and indeed his direct debts are limited to a few scattered phrases, as in the Ballad of Dowsabel. Almost to the end of his literary career, Drayton mentions Spenser with reverence and praise.

It is in the songs interspersed in the Eclogues that Drayton's best work at this time is to be found: already his metrical versatility is discernible; for though he doubtless remembered the many varieties of metre employed by Spenser in the Calendar, his verses already bear a stamp of their own. The long but impetuous lines, such as 'Trim up her golden tresses with Apollo's sacred tree', afford a striking contrast to the archaic romance-metre, derived from Sir Thopas and its fellows, which appears in Dowsabel, and it again to the melancholy, murmuring cadences of the lament for Elphin. It must, however, be confessed that certain of the songs in the 1593 edition were full of recondite conceits and laboured antitheses, and were rightly struck out, to be replaced by lovelier poems, in the edition of 1606. The song to Beta was printed in Englands Helicon, 1600; here, for the first time, appeared the song of Dead Love, and for the only time, Rowlands Madrigal. In these songs, Drayton offends least in grammar, always a weak point with him; in the body of the Eclogues, in the earlier Sonnets, in the Odes, occur the most extraordinary and perplexing inversions. Quite the most striking feature of the Eclogues, especially in their later form, is their bold attempt at greater realism, at a breaking-away from the conventional images and scenery.

Having paid his tribute to one poetic fashion, Drayton in 1594 fell in with the prevailing craze for sonneteering, and published Ideas Mirrour, a series of fifty-one 'amours' or sonnets, with two prefatory poems, one by Drayton and one by an unknown, signing himself Gorbo il fidele. The title of these poems

Drayton possibly borrowed from the French sonneteer, de Pontoux: in their style much recollection of Sidney, Constable, and Daniel is traceable. They are ostensibly addressed to his mistress, and some of them are genuine in feeling; but many are merely imitative exercises in conceit; some, apparently, trials in metre. These amours were again printed, with the title of 'sonnets', in 1599, 1600, 1602, 1603, 1605, 1608, 1610, 1613, 1619, and 1631, during the poet's lifetime. It is needless here to discuss whether Drayton were the 'rival poet' to Shakespeare, whether these sonnets were really addressed to a man, or merely to the ideal Platonic beauty; for those who are interested in these points, I subjoin references to the sonnets which touch upon them. From the prentice-work evident in many of the Amours, it would seem that certain of them are among Drayton's earliest poems; but others show a craftsman not meanly advanced in his art. Nevertheless, with few exceptions, this first 'bundle of sonnets' consists rather of trials of skill, bubbles of the mind; most of his sonnets which strike the reader as touched or penetrated with genuine passion belong to the editions from 1599 onwards; implying that his love for Anne Goodere, if at all represented in these poems, grew with his years, for the 'love-parting' is first found in the edition of 1619. But for us the question should not be, are these sonnets genuine representations of the personal feeling of the poet? but rather, how far do they arouse or echo in us as individuals the universal passion? There are at least some of Drayton's sonnets which possess a direct, instant, and universal appeal, by reason of their simple force and straightforward ring; and not in virtue of any subtle charm of sound and rhythm, or overmastering splendour of diction or thought. Ornament vanishes, and soberness and simplicity increase, as we proceed in the editions of the sonnets. Drayton's chief attempt in the jewelled or ornamental style appeared in 1595, with the title of Endimion and Phoebe, and was, in a sense, an imitation of Marlowe's Hero and Leander. Hero and Leander is, as Swinburne says, a shrine of Parian marble, illumined from within by a clear flame of passion; while Endimion and Phoebe is rather a curiously wrought tapestry, such as that in Mortimer's Tower, woven in splendid and harmonious colours, wherein, however, the figures attain no clearness or subtlety of outline, and move in semi-conventional scenery. It is, none the less, graceful and impressive, and of a like musical fluency with other poems of its class, such as Venus and Adonis, or Salmacis and Hermaphrodius. Parts of it were re-set and spoilt in a 1606 publication of Drayton's, called The Man in the Moone.

In 1593 and 1594 Drayton also published his earliest pieces on the mediaeval theme of the 'Falls of the Illustrious'; they were Peirs Gavesson and Matilda the faire and chaste daughter of the Lord Robert Fitzwater. Here Drayton followed in the track of Boccaccio, Lydgate, and the Mirrour for Magistrates, walking in the way which Chaucer had derided in his Monkes Tale: and with only too great fidelity does Drayton adapt himself to the dullnesses of his model: fine rhetoric is not altogether wanting, and there is, of course, the consciousness that these subjects deal with the history of his beloved country, but neither these, nor Robert, Duke of Normandy (1596), nor Great Cromwell, Earl of Essex (1607 and 1609), nor the Miseries of Margaret (1627) can escape the charge of tediousness. England's Heroical Epistles were first published in 1597, and other editions, of 1598, 1599, and 1602, contain new epistles. These are Drayton's first attempt to strike out a new and original vein of English poetry: they are a series of letters, modelled on Ovid's Heroides, addressed by various pairs of lovers, famous in English history, to each other, and arranged in chronological order, from Henry II and Rosamond to Lady Jane Grey and Lord Guilford Dudley. They are, in a sense, the most important of Drayton's writings, and they have certainly been the most popular, up to the early nineteenth century. In these poems Drayton foreshadowed, and probably inspired, the smooth style of Fairfax, Waller, and Dryden. The metre, the grammar, and the thought, are all perfectly easy to follow, even though he employs many of the Ovidian 'turns' and 'clenches'. A certain attempt at realization of the different characters is observable, but the poems are fine rhetorical exercises rather than realizations of the dramatic and passionate possibilities of their themes. In 1596, Drayton, as we have seen, published the Mortimeriados, a kind of epic, with Mortimer as its hero, of the wars between King Edward II and the Barons. It was written in the seven-line stanza of Chaucer's Troilus and Cressida and Spenser's Hymns. On its republication in 1603, with the title of the Barons' Wars, the metre was changed to ottava rima, and Drayton showed, in an excellent preface, that he fully appreciated the principles and the subtleties of the metrical art. While possessing many fine passages, the Barons' Wars is somewhat dull, lacking much of the poetry of the older version; and does not escape from Drayton's own criticism of Daniel's Chronicle Poems: 'too much historian in verse, ... His rhymes were smooth, his metres well did close, But yet his manner better fitted prose'. The description of Mortimer's Tower in the sixth book recalls the ornate style of Endimion and Phoebe, while the fifth book, describing the miseries of King Edward, is the most moving and dramatic. But there is a general lifelessness and lack of movement for which these purple passages barely atone. The cause of the production of so many chronicle poems about this time has been supposed to be the desire of showing the horrors of civil war, at a time when the queen was growing old, and no successor had, as it seemed, been accepted. Also they were a kind of parallel to the Chronicle Play; and Drayton, in any case even if we grant him to have been influenced by the example of Daniel, never needed much incentive to treat a national theme.

About this time, we find Drayton writing for the stage. It seems unnecessary here to discuss whether the writing of plays is evidence of Drayton's poverty, or his versatility; but the fact remains that he had a hand in the production of about twenty. Of these, the only one which certainly survives is The first part of the true and honorable historie, of the life of Sir John Oldcastle, the good Lord Cobham, &c. It is practically impossible to distinguish Drayton's share in this curious play, and it does not, therefore, materially assist the elucidation of the question whether he had any dramatic feeling or skill. It can be safely affirmed that the dramatic instinct was nor uppermost in his mind; he was a Seneca rather than a Euripides: but to deny him all dramatic idea, as does Dr. Whitaker, is too severe. There is decided, if slender, dramatic skill and feeling in certain of the Nymphals. Drayton's persons are usually, it must be said, rather figures in a tableau, or series of tableaux; but in the second and seventh Nymphals, and occasionally in the tenth, there is real dramatic movement. Closely connected with this question is the consideration of humour, which is wrongly denied to Drayton. Humour is observable first, perhaps, in the Owle (1604); then in the Ode to his Rival (1619); and later in the Nymphidia, Shepheards Sirena, and Muses Elyzium. The second Nymphal shows us the quiet laughter, the humorous twinkle, with which Drayton writes at times. The subject is an [Greek: agôn] or contest between two shepherds for the affections of a nymph called Lirope: Lalus is a vale-bred swain, of refined and elegant manners, skilled, nevertheless, in all manly sports and exercises; Cleon, no less a master in physical prowess, was nurtured by a hind in the mountains; the contrast between their manners is admirably sustained: Cleon is rough, inclined to be rude and scoffing, totally without tact, even where his mistress is concerned. Lalus remembers her upbringing and her tastes; he makes no unnecessary or ostentatious display of wealth; his gifts are simple and charming, while Cleon's are so grotesquely unsuited to a swain, that it is tempting to suppose that Drayton was quietly satirizing Marlowe's Passionate Shepherd. Lirope listens gravely to the swains in turn, and makes demure but provoking answers, raising each to the height of hope, and then casting them both down into the depths of despair; finally she refuses both, yet without altogether killing hope. Her first answer is a good specimen of her banter and of Drayton's humour.

On the accession of James I, Drayton hastened to greet the King with a somewhat laboured song To the Maiestie of King James; but this poem was apparently considered to be premature: he cried Vivat Rex, without having said, Mortua est eheu Regina, and accordingly he suffered the penalty of his 'forward pen', and was severely neglected by King and Court. Throughout James's reign a darker and more satirical mood possesses Drayton, intruding at times even into his strenuous recreation-ground, the Poly-Olbion, and manifesting itself more directly in his satires, the Owle (1604), the Moon-Calfe (1627), the Man in the Moone (1606), and his verse-letters and elegies; while his disappointment with the times, the country, and the King, flashes out occasionally even in the Odes, and is heard in his last publication, the Muses Elizium (1630). To counterbalance the disappointment in his hopes from the King, Drayton found a new and life-long friend in Walter Aston, of Tixall, in Staffordshire; this gentleman was created Knight of the Bath by James, and made Drayton one of his esquires. By Aston's 'continual bounty' the poet was able to devote himself almost entirely to more congenial literary work; for, while Meres speaks of the Poly-Olbion in 1598, and we may easily see that Drayton had the idea of that work at least as early as 1594, yet he cannot have been able to give much time to it till now. Nevertheless, the 'declining and corrupt times' worked on Drayton's mind and grieved and darkened his soul, for we must remember that he was perfectly prosperous then and was not therefore incited to satire by bodily want or distress.

In 1604 he published the Owle, a mild satire, under the form of a moral fable of government, reminding the reader a little of the Parlement of Foules. The Man in the Moone (1606) is partly a recension of Endimion and Phoebe, but is a heterogeneous mass of weakly satire, of no particular merit. The Moon-Calfe (1627) is Drayton's most savage and misanthropic excursion into the region of Satire; in which, though occasionally nobly ironic, he is more usually coarse and blustering, in the style of Marston. In 1605 Drayton brought out his first 'collected poems', from which the Eclogues and the Owle are omitted; and in 1606 he published his Poemes Lyrick and Pastorall, Odes, Eglogs, The Man in the Moone. Of these the Eglogs are a recension of the Shepherd's Garland of 1593: we have already spoken of The Man in the Moone. The Odes are by far the most important and striking feature of the book. In the preface, Drayton professes to be following Pindar, Anacreon, and Horace, though, as he modestly implies, at a great distance. Under the title of Odes he includes a variety of subjects, and a variety of metres; ranging from an Ode to his Harp or to his Criticks, to a Ballad of Agincourt, or a poem on the Rose compared with his Mistress. In the edition of 1619 appeared several more Odes, including some of the best; while many of the others underwent careful revision, notably the Ballad. 'Sing wee the Rose,' perhaps because of its unintelligibility, and the Ode to his friend John Savage, perhaps because too closely imitated from Horace, were omitted. Drayton was not the first to use the term Ode for a lyrical poem, in English: Soothern in 1584, and Daniel in 1592 had preceded him; but he was the first to give the name popularity in England, and to lift the kind as Ronsard had lifted it in France; and till the time of Cowper no other English poet showed mastery of the short, staccato measure of the Anacreontic as distinct from the Pindaric Ode. In the Odes Drayton shows to the fullest extent his metrical versatility: he touches the Skeltonic metre, the long ten-syllabled line of the Sacrifice to Apollo; and ascends from the smooth and melodious rhythms of the New Year through the inspiring harp-tones of the Virginian Voyage to the clangour and swing of the Ballad of Agincourt. His grammar is possibly more distorted here than anywhere, but, as Mr. Elton says, 'these are the obstacles of any poet who uses measures of four or six syllables.' His tone throughout is rather that of the harp, as played, perhaps, in Polesworth Hall, than that of any other instrument; but in 1619 Drayton has taken to him the lute of Carew and his compeers. In 1619 the style is lighter, the fancy gayer, more exquisite, more recondite. Most of his few metaphysical conceits are to be found in these later Odes, as in the Heart, the Valentine, and the Crier. In the comparison of the two editions the nobler, if more strained, tone of the earlier is obvious; it is still Elizabethan, in its nobility of ideal and purpose, in its enthusiasm, in its belief and confidence in England and her men; and this even though we catch a glimpse of the Jacobean woe in the Ode to John Savage: the 1619 Odes are of a different world; their spirit is lighter, more insouciant in appearance, though perhaps studiedly so; the rhythms are more fantastic, with less of strength and firmness, though with more of grace and superficial beauty; even the very textual alterations, while usually increasing the grace and the music of the lines, remind the reader that something of the old spontaneity and freshness is gone.

In 1607 and 1609, Drayton published two editions of the last and weakest of his mediaeval poems—the Legend of Great Cromwell; and for the next few years he produced nothing new, only attending to the publication of certain reprints and new editions. During this time, however, he was working steadily at the Poly-Olbion, helped by the patronage of Aston and of Prince Henry. In 1612-13, Drayton burst upon an indifferent world with the first part of the great poem, containing eighteen songs; the title-page will give the best idea of the contents and plan of the book: 'Poly-Olbion or a Chorographicall Description of the Tracts, Riuers, Mountaines, Forests, and other Parts of this renowned Isle of Great Britaine, With intermixture of the most Remarquable Stories, Antiquities, Wonders, Rarityes, Pleasures, and Commodities of the same: Digested in a Poem by Michael Drayton, Esq. With a Table added, for direction to those occurrences of Story and Antiquities, whereunto the Course of the Volume easily leades not.' &c. On this work Drayton had been engaged for nearly the whole of his poetical career. The learning and research displayed in the poem are extraordinary, almost equalling the erudition of Selden in his Annotations to each Song. The first part was, for various reasons, a drug in the market, and Drayton found great difficulty in securing a publisher for the second part. But during the years from 1613 to 1622, he became acquainted with Drummond of Hawthornden through a common friend, Sir William Alexander of Menstry, afterwards Earl of Stirling. In 1618, Drayton starts a correspondence; and towards the end of the year mentions that he is corresponding also with Andro Hart, bookseller, of Edinburgh. The subject of his letter was probably the publication of the Second Part; which Drayton alludes to in a letter of 1619 thus: 'I have done twelve books more, that is from the eighteenth book, which was Kent, if you note it; all the East part and North to the river Tweed; but it lies by me; for the booksellers and I are in terms; they are a company of base knaves, whom I both scorn and kick at.' Finally, in 1622, Drayton got Marriott, Grismand, and Dewe, of London, to take the work, and it was published with a dedication to Prince Charles, who, after his brother's death, had given Drayton patronage. Drayton's preface to the Second Part is well worth quoting:

'To any that will read it. When I first undertook this Poem, or, as some very skilful in this kind have pleased to term it, this Herculean labour, I was by some virtuous friends persuaded, that I should receive much comfort and encouragement therein; and for these reasons; First, that it was a new, clear, way, never before gone by any; then, that it contained all the Delicacies, Delights, and Rarities of this renowned Isle, interwoven with the Histories of the Britons, Saxons, Normans, and the later English: And further that there is scarcely any of the Nobility or Gentry of this land, but that he is in some way or other by his Blood interested therein. But it hath fallen out otherwise; for instead of that comfort, which my noble friends (from the freedom of their spirits) proposed as my due, I have met with barbarous ignorance, and base detraction; such a cloud hath the Devil drawn over the world's judgment, whose opinion is in few years fallen so far below all ballatry, that the lethargy is incurable: nay, some of the Stationers, that had the selling of the First Part of this Poem, because it went not so fast away in the sale, as some of their beastly and abominable trash, (a shame both to our language and nation) have either despitefully left out, or at least carelessly neglected the Epistles to the Readers, and so have cozened the buyers with unperfected books; which these that have undertaken the Second Part, have been forced to amend in the First, for the small number that are yet remaining in their hands. And some of our outlandish, unnatural, English, (I know not how otherwise to express them) stick not to say that there is nothing in this Island worth studying for, and take a great pride to be ignorant in any thing thereof; for these, since they delight in their folly, I wish it may be hereditary from them to their posterity, that their children may be begg'd for fools to the fifth generation, until it may be beyond the memory of man to know that there was ever other of their families: neither can this deter me from going on with Scotland, if means and time do not hinder me, to perform as much as I have promised in my First Song:

Till through the sleepy main, to Thuly I have gone,
And seen the Frozen Isles, the cold Deucalidon,
Amongst whose iron Rocks, grim Saturn yet remains
Bound in those gloomy caves with adamantine chains.

And as for those cattle whereof I spake before, Odi profanum vulgus, et arceo, of which I account them,
be they never so great, and so I leave them. To my friends, and the lovers of my labours, I wish all
happiness.
Michael Drayton.'

The Poly-Olbion as a whole is easy and pleasant to read; and though in some parts it savours too much
of a mere catalogue, yet it has many things truly poetical. The best books are perhaps the XIII, XIV and
XV, where he is on his own ground, and therefore naturally at his best. It is interesting to notice how
much attention and space he devotes to Wales. He describes not only the 'wonders' but also the fauna
and flora of each district; and of the two it would seem that the flowers interested him more. Though he
was a keen observer of country sights and sounds (a fact sufficiently attested by the Nymphidia and the
Nymphals), it is evident that his interest in most things except flowers was rather momentary or
conventional than continuous and heart-felt; but of the flowers he loves to talk, whether he weaves us a
garland for the Thame's wedding, or gives us the contents of a maund of simples; and his love, if
somewhat homely and unimaginative, is apparent enough. But the main inspiration, as it is the main
theme, of the Poly-Olbion is the glory and might and wealth, past, present, and future, of England, her
possessions and her folk. Through all this glory, however, we catch the tone of Elizabethan sorrow over
the 'Ruines of Time'; grief that all these mighty men and their works will perish and be forgotten, unless
the poet makes them live for ever on the lips of men. Drayton's own voluminousness has defeated his
purpose, and sunk his poem by its own bulk. Though it is difficult to go so far as Mr. Bullen, and say that
the only thing better than a stroll in the Poly-Olbion is one in a Sussex lane, it is still harder to agree with
Canon Beeching, that 'there are few beauties on the road', the beauties are many, though of a quietly
rural type, and the road, if long and winding, is of good surface, while its cranks constitute much of its
charm. It is doubtless, from the outside, an appalling poem in these days of epitomes and monographs,
but it certainly deserves to be rescued from oblivion and read.

In 1618 Drayton contributed two Elegies to Henry FitzGeoffrey's Satyrs and Epigrames. These were on
the Lady Penelope Clifton, and on 'the death of the three sonnes of the Lord Sheffield, drowned neere
where Trent falleth into Humber'. Neither is remarkable save for far-fetched conceits; they were
reprinted in 1610, and again, with many others, in the volume of 1627. In 1619 Drayton issued a folio
collected edition of his works, and reprinted it in 1620. In 1627 followed a folio of wholly fresh matter,
including the Battaile of Agincourt; the Miseries of Queene Margarite, Nimphidia, Quest of Cinthia,
Shepheards Sirena, Moone-Calfe, and Elegies upon sundry occasions. The Battaile of Agincourt is a
somewhat otiose expansion, with purple patches, of the Ballad; it is, nevertheless, Drayton's best
lengthy piece on a historical theme. Of the Miseries of Queene Margarite and of the Moone-Calfe we
have already spoken. The most notable piece in the book is the Nimphidia. This poem of the Court of
Fairy has 'invention, grace, and humour', as Canon Beeching has said. It would be interesting to know
exactly when it was composed and committed to paper, for it is thought that the three fairy poems in
Herrick's Hesperides were written about 1626. In any case, Drayton's poem touches very little, and
chiefly in the beginning, on the subject of any one of Herrick's three pieces. The style, execution, and
impression left on the reader are quite different; even as they are totally unlike those of the Midsummer
Night's Dream. Herrick's pieces are extraordinary combinations of the idea of 'King of Shadows', with a
reality fantastically sober: the poems are steeped in moonlight. In Drayton all is clear day, or the most

unromantic of nights; though everything is charming, there is no attempt at idealization, little of the higher faculty of imagination; but great realism, and much play of fancy. Herrick's verses were written by Cobweb and Moth together, Drayton's by Puck. Granting, however, the initial deficiency in subtlety of charm, the whole poem is inimitably graceful and piquant. The gay humour, the demure horror of the witchcraft, the terrible seriousness of the battle, wonderfully realize the mock-heroic gigantesque; and while there is not the minute accuracy of Gulliver in Lilliput, Drayton did not write for a sceptical or too-prying audience; quite half his readers believed more or less in fairies. In the metre of the poem Drayton again echoes that of the older romances, as he did in Dowsabel. In the Quest of Cinthia, while ostensibly we come to the real world of mortals, we are really in a non-existent land of pastoral convention, in the most pseudo-Arcadian atmosphere in which Drayton ever worked. The metre and the language are, however, charmingly managed. The Shepheards Sirena is a poem, apparently, 'where more is meant than meets the ear,' as so often in pastoral poetry; it is difficult to see exactly what is meant; but the Jacobean strain of doubt and fear is there, and the poem would seem to have been written some time earlier than 1627. The Elegies comprise a great variety of styles and themes; some are really threnodies, some verse-letters, some laments over the evil times, and one a summary of Drayton's literary opinions. He employs the couplet in his Elegies with a masterly hand, often with a deliberately rugged effect, as in his broader Marstonic satire addressed to William Browne; while the line of greater smoothness but equal strength is to be seen in the letters to Sandys and Jeffreys. He is fantastic and conceited in most of the threnodies; but, as is natural, that on his old friend, Sir Henry Raynsford, is least artificial and fullest of true feeling. The epistle to Henery Reynolds. Of Poets and Poesie shows Drayton as a sane and sagacious critic, ready to see the good, but keen to discern the weakness also; perhaps the clearest evidence of his critical skill is the way in which nearly all of his judgements on his contemporaries coincide with the received modern opinions.

In his later years Drayton enjoyed the patronage of the third Earl and Countess of Dorset; and in 1630 he published his last volume, the Muses Elizium, of which he dedicated the pastoral part to the Earl, and the three divine poems at the end to the Countess. The Muses Elizium proper consists of Ten Pastorals or Nymphals, prefaced by a Description of Elizium. The three divine poems have been mentioned before, and were Noah's Floud, Moses his Birth and Miracles, and David and Goliah. The Nymphals are the crown and summary of much of the best in Drayton's work. Here he departed from the conventional type of pastoral, even more than in the Shepherd's Garland; but to say that he sang of English rustic life would hardly be true: the sixth Nymphal, allowing for a few pardonable exaggerations by the competitors, is almost all English, if we except the names; so is the tenth with the same exception; the first and fourth might take place anywhere, but are not likely in any country; the second is more conventional; the fifth is almost, but not quite, English; the third, seventh, and ninth are avowedly classical in theme; while the eighth is a more delicate and subtle fairy poem than the Nymphidia. The fourth and tenth Nymphals are also touched with the sadder, almost satiric vein; the former inveighing against the English imitation of foreigners and love of extravagance in dress; while the tenth complains of the improvident and wasteful felling of trees in the English forests. This last Nymphal, though designedly an epilogue, is probably rather a warning than a despairing lament, even though we conceive the old satyr to be Drayton himself. As a whole the Nymphals show Drayton at his happiest and lightest in style and metre; at his moments of greatest serenity and even gaiety; an atmosphere of sunshine seems to envelope them all, though the sun sink behind a cloud in the last. His music now is that of a rippling stream, whereas in his earlier days he spoke weightier and more sonorous words, with a mouth of gold.

To estimate the poetical faculty of Drayton is a somewhat perplexing task; for, while rarely subtle, or rising to empyrean heights, he wrote in such varied styles, on such various themes, that the task, at first, seems that of criticizing many poets, not one. But through all his work runs the same eminently English spirit, the same honesty and clearness of idea, the same stolidity of purpose, and not infrequently of execution also; the same enthusiasm characterizes all his earlier, and much of his later work; the enthusiasm especially characteristic of Elizabethan England, and shown by Drayton in his passion for England and the English, in his triumphant joy in their splendid past, and his certainty of their future glory. As a poet, he lacked imagination and fine fury; he supplied their place by the airiest and clearest of fancies, by the strenuous labour of a great brain illumined by the steady flame of love for his country and for his lady. Mr. Courthope has said that he lacked loftiness and resolution of artistic purpose; without these, we ask, how could a man, not lavishly dowered with poetry in his soul, have achieved so much of it? It was his very fixity and loftiness of purpose, his English stubbornness and doggedness of resolution that enabled him to surmount so many obstacles of style and metre, of subject and thought. His two purposes, of glorifying his mistress and his friends, and of sounding England's glories past and future, while insisting on the dangers of a present decadence, never flagged or failed. All his poetry up to 1627 has this object directly or secondarily; and much after this date. Of the more abstract and universal aspects of his art he had not much conception; but he caught eagerly at the fashionable belief in the eternizing power of poetry; and had it not been that, where his patriotism was uppermost, he was deficient in humour and sense of proportion, he would have succeeded better: as it is, his more directly patriotic pieces are usually the dullest or longest of his works. He requires, like all other poets, the impulse of an absolutely personal and individual feeling, a moment of more intimate sympathy, to rouse him to his heights of song. Thus the Ballad of Agincourt is on the very theme of all patriotic themes that most attracted him; Virginian and other Voyages lay very close to his heart; and in certain sonnets to his lady lies his only imperishable work. Of sheer melody and power of song he had little, apart from his themes: he could not have sat down and written a few lark's or nightingale's notes about nothing as some of his contemporaries were able to do: he required the stimulus of a subject, and if he were really moved thereby he beat the music out. Only in one or two of the later Odes, and in the volumes of 1627 and 1630, does his music ever seem to flow from him naturally. Akin to this quality of broad and extensive workmanship, to this faculty of taking a subject and when writing, with all thought concentrated on it, rather than on the method of writing about it, is his strange lack of what are usually called 'quotations'. For this is not only due to the fact that he is little known; there are, besides, so few detached remarks or aphorisms that are separately quotable; so few examples of that curiosa felicitas of diction: lines like these,

Thy Bowe, halfe broke, is peec'd with old desire;
Her Bowe is beauty with ten thousand strings....

are rare enough. Drayton, in fact, comes as near controverting the statement Poeta nascitur, non fit, as any one in English literature: by diligent toil and earnest desire he won a place for himself in the second rank of English poets: through love he once set foot in the circle of the mightiest. Sincere he was always, simple often, sensuous rarely. His great industry, his careful study, and his great receptivity are shown in the unusual spectacle of a man who has sung well in the language of his youth, suddenly learning, in his age, the tongue spoken by the younger generation, and reproducing it with individuality and sureness of touch. It is in rhetoric, splendid or rugged, in argument, in plain statement or description, in the outline sketch of a picture, that Drayton excels; magic of atmosphere and colouring are rarely present. Stolidity is, perhaps, his besetting sin; yet it is the sign of a slow, not a dull, intellect; an intellect, like his heart, which never let slip what it had once taken to itself.

As a man Drayton would seem to have been an excellent type of the sturdy, clear-headed, but yet romantic and enthusiastic Englishman; gifted with much natural ability, sedulously increased by study;

quietly humorous, self-restrained; and if temporarily soured by disappointment and the disjointed times, yet emerging at last into a greater serenity, a more unadulterated gaiety than had ever before characterized him. It is possible, but from his clear and sane balance of mind improbable, that many of his light later poems are due to deliberate self-blinding and self-deception, a walking in enchanted lands of the mind.

Of Drayton's three known portraits the earliest shows him at the age of thirty-six, and is now in the National Portrait Gallery. A look of quiet, speculative melancholy seems to pervade it; there is, as yet, no moroseness, no evidence of severe conflict with the world, no shadow of stress or of doubt. The second and best-known portrait shows us Drayton at the age of fifty, and was engraved by Hole, as a frontispiece to the poems of 1619. Here a notable change has come over the face; the mouth is hardened, and depressed at the corners through disappointment and disillusionment; the eyes are full of a pathos increased by the puzzled and perturbed uplift of the brows. Yet a stubbornness and tenacity of purpose invests the features and reminds us that Drayton is of the old and sound Elizabethan stock, 'on evil days though fallen.' Let it be remembered, that he was in 1613, when the portrait was taken, in more or less prosperous circumstances; it was the sad degeneracy, the meanness and feebleness of the generation around him, that chiefly depressed and embittered him. The final portrait, now in the Dulwich Gallery, represents the poet as a man of sixty-five; and is quite in keeping with the sunnier and calmer tone of his later poetry. It is the face of one who has not emerged unscathed from the world's conflict, but has attained to a certain calm, a measure of tranquillity, a portion of content, who has learnt the lesson that there is a soul of goodness in things evil. The Hole portrait shows him with long hair, small 'goatee' beard, and aquiline nose drawn up at the nostrils: while the National portrait shows a type of nose and beard intermediate between the Hole and the Dulwich pictures: the general contour of the face, though the forehead is broad enough, is long and oval. Drayton seems to have been tall and thin, and to have been very susceptible of cold, and therefore to have hated Winter and the North. He is said to have shared in the supper which caused Shakespeare's death; but his own verses breathe the spirit of Milton's sonnet to Cyriack Skinner, rather than that of a devotee of Bacchus.

He died in 1631, probably December 23, and was buried under the North wall of Westminster Abbey. Meres's opinion of his character during his early life is as follows: 'As Aulus Persius Flaccus is reported among al writers to be of an honest life and vpright conuersation: so Michael Drayton, quem toties honoris et amoris causa nomino, among schollers, souldiours, Poets, and all sorts of people is helde for a man of uertuous disposition, honest conversation, and well gouerned cariage; which is almost miraculous among good wits in these declining and corrupt times, when there is nothing but rogery in villanous man, and when cheating and craftines is counted the cleanest wit, and soundest wisedome.' Fuller also, in a similar strain, says, 'He was a pious poet, his conscience having the command of his fancy, very temperate in his life, slow of speech, and inoffensive in company.'

A Chronology of Michael Drayton's Life and Works

1563	Drayton born at Hartshill, Warwickshire.
c. 1572	Drayton a page in the house of Sir Henry Goodere, at Polesworth.
c. 1574	Anne Goodere born
February, 1591	Drayton in London. Harmony of Church.
1593	Idea, the Shepherd's Garland. Legend of Peirs Gaveston.
1594	Ideas Mirrour. Matilda. Lucy Harrington becomes Countess of Bedford.

1595	Sir Henry Goodere the elder dies. Endimion and Phoebe, dedicated to Lucy Bedford.
1595-6	Anne Goodere married to Sir Henry Raynsford.
1596	Mortimeriados. Legends of Robert, Matilda, and Gaveston.
1597	England's Heroical Epistles.
1598	Drayton already at work on the Poly-Olbion.
1599	Epistles and Idea sonnets, new edition. (Date of Drayton portrait in National Portrait Gallery.)
1600	Sir John Oldcastle.
1602	New edition of Epistles and Idea.
1603	Drayton made an Esquire of the Bath, to Sir Walter Aston. To the Maiestie of King James. Barons' Wars.
1604	The Owle. A Pean Triumphall. Moyses in a Map of his Miracles.
1605	First collected edition of Poems. Another edition of Idea and Epistles.
1606	Poemes Lyrick and Pastorall. Odes. Eglogs. The Man in the Moone.
1607	Legend of Great Cromwell.
1608	Reprint of Collected Poems.
1609	Another edition of Cromwell.
1610	Reprint of Collected Poems.
1613	Reprint of Collected Poems. First Part of Poly-Olbion.
1618	Two Elegies in FitzGeoffrey's Satyrs and Epigrames.
1619	Collected Folio edition of Poems.
1620	Second edition of Elegies, and reprint of 1619 Poems.
1622	Poly-Olbion complete.
1627	Battle of Agincourt, Nymphidia, &c.
1630	Muses Elizium. Noah's Floud. Moses his Birth and Miracles. David and Goliah.
1631	Second edition of 1627 folio. Drayton dies December 23rd.
1636	Posthumous poem appeared in Annalia Dubrensia.
1637	Poems.

Michael Drayton – A Concise Bibliography

The Major Works

The Harmony of the Church (1591)
Idea, The Shepherd's Garland (1593)
Idea's Mirror (1594)
Peirs Gaveston (1593 or 1594)
Matilda (1594)
Endimion and Phoebe: Idea's Latmus (1595)
The Tragical Legend of Robert, Duke of Normandy (1596)
Mortimeriados (1596)
England's Heroicall Epistles (1597)
The First Part of the Life of Sir John Oldcastle (1600)
The Barons' Wars in the Reign of Edward II (1603)
The Owl (1604)
The Man in the Moon (1606)

The Legend of Thomas Cromwell, Earl of Essex (1607)
Poly-Olbion (1612 & 1622)
Idea (1619)
Pastorals: Containing Eclogues (1619)
Odes (1619)
The Battle of Agincourt (published 1627)
The Quest of Cynthia (published 1627)
Elegies Upon Sundry Occasions (1627)
Nymphidia, the Court of Fairy (1627)
The Shepherd's Sirena (1627)
Muses' Elysium (1630)
Moses' Birth and Miracles (1630)

www.ingramcontent.com/pod-product-compliance
Lightning Source LLC
Chambersburg PA
CBHW060145050426
42448CB00010B/2306